Political FiddleFaddle

Jake Street

ISBN: 153275907X
ISBN-13: 9781532759079

DEDICATION

To the long suffering
who have listened
for years to the rants and sermons
on the subjects or issues herein.
And to those kindred souls
who will find
reinforcement and justification
of their own rants and sermons herein…

You are not alone

We're just outnumbered.

CONTENTS

FORWARD

A Forward is much like an accordion which, a music lover observed, is not much good for anything, and should be avoided at all times.

But a book, especially, one with parts of it originally scribbled down during or over a quarter of a century, needs some sort of a forward; an introduction, for several reasons.

The main reason why a forward is needed here, is to warn some potential readers that "inserts" and "updates" have been added – as well as some "told you so's" about a few events that we said back then *would* occur.

Overall, without echoing far-out theories from fuzzy minds, we compare what our economic leaders have said and done to what our economy has achieved over the last half-century.

Voters have a lot to answer for...

We have idiots – in both national parties – who keep telling us that we can spend our way to prosperity by adding more debt. And we elect and re-elect and re-elect and re-elect and re-elect these idiots to office.

We do it because we blindly claim "we're democrats" or "republicans" or "libertarians".

But that is only partially true.

The real reason we do it is because we are bigger idiots than the ones we elect to office.

The ones we elect and re-elect are smart enough to grow rich and powerful on our stupidity.

The good ol' USA is heading in the wrong direction. We are a nation that seems to have lost its purpose. America is straying from its objective and is setting goals that will lead to economic destruction.

And if we are not there yet, you can see it coming from your kitchen window.

Today, too many generations are being force fed centralized nonsense. Instead of feeding in a brave new world, we are, under a new label of State Capitalism, greedily gobbling down the regurgitated garbage of old-world socialism.

Back then, like today, the thought began to seep into our skulls that most politicians are proven wrong about whatever it was they had been yakking about. A number of revolts and civil wars were the results.

Generally, today, there is a grab-bag of stuff that politicians and those pushing special agendas can reach into and pull out something that glitters and they can "point to with pride or view with alarm." It is a confusing blabber about jobs, wages, unemployment, inflation, stagnation, debt, investment, productivity, foreign markets, regulations, the stock market, and a hundred other things of interest to *the government.*

And as Willie said, "Ah, there's the rub."

Constitutional restraints on our government, and on people are lost in the things that government wants control over; things that are, therefore, important to government.

It is about categories: placing large segments of society into some classifications and cataloging them into manageable portions.

It is about squeaky wheel things that government can spill a little grease on and, in turn, the squeaky wheel owes the government its thanks – and its allegiance.

It is about politicians talking about things they have little to no knowledge of, such as how to create a worthwhile job, control inflation, or how to make our lives better.

We were told times have changed. And that America needed to change with it. And that only government could understand this big, exotic, esoteric change thing, and that only government could accomplish it, and that more government would improve our day-to-day lives.

It is about control.

And we bought it.

We confused our Constitution with politics.

We surrendered (gave) our Constitutional protection to the government planners.

And the administrators of the resulting government programs started moving us farther and farther away from the greatest economic system the world has ever known. And the result is a nation in even more economic turmoil than in the 1990s; more confused about how we got here, who we are, and still asking where we are headed.

So, here, are some odds-and-ends that examine why we are a nation that benefits a few, but that is of relatively little benefit to millions of working men and women busting their butts to put food on the table, clothes on their backs, or a roof over their heads.

And numerous questions why we are *forced* by our government to guarantee a profit for a privileged few insiders, doing quite well from management fees and the big bonus, while a slumping dollar means we and working families must expend more energy just to stay even.

Most of all, we want to know why there is no equal treatment under the law – as mandated in the U. S. Constitution.

1 MESSIN' UP . . .

The legions of experts, political and news media, whom we trusted to explain complex economic and financial matters, and who have rained remedies like snowflakes on us, buried us in remedies, have completely failed us.

Repeatedly, we're barraged by hokum, wrapped up in Happy Talk, that our government and it's gift of high unemployment, soaring government debt, collapsed real estate markets, a failing banking system, a financial system that wouldn't support a gnat, and a host of other negative workings, which will see us thru (at least, until Friday).

It is the lies and misinformation-by-misinformation experts, mouthed by mass media know-nothings happy in their stupidity.

Most of us never seem to realize that it was government (those in government), who created the mess we are in by destroying the greatest economic system the world has ever known.

America is not America anymore. The Dream is lost in political correctness and false assumptions.

The truth is that, if we continue on our recent course, a lot of countries engaged in State Capitalism are going down for the count.

The Happy Talkers are also giving us hokum about the type of economic restructuring America now needs, and that is so difficult and painful, they say, that it will take many years to do. What the message really means is that placing the remaining economic power of the big businesses and financial institutions under total government control will demand some sacrifice for 90% of all Americans.

You cannot achieve a nation of the United Socialists States of America without the individual sacrifice demanded by the courage of the mentally deranged.

Oh, of course, there are those Americans-in-name-only who believe the idea that our brand of centralized government is different from that of the world's other centralized governments.

Too many of us have an eager and naïve willingness to find reassurance in the Happy Talk we are forced-fed.

We have listened to shamans and shysters and accepted the unholy mess they got us in, and any hope that it will all turn out well is slim to non-existent.

The restructuring America needs is simple: Return to a private enterprise system of asset based lending by banks.

The key word being "banks" – not the huge, flawed, "financial institutions" we created in the 1980s. These insurance peddling, stock brokering and feather-nesting things are not banks. They are politically-created-for-pay vehicles that collect big fees on big financial deals for a few key insiders.

And the mergers, takeovers, buyouts, and multi-billion dollar startups – all the "big deals" – are guaranteed against failure by the federally-centralized government.

It is pure State Capitalism, an economic system for the 5,000 or so more actively traded conglomerates in the New York, American, and NASDAQ stock markets.

Until the last 50-or so years, America's economic system was one of individual choice with equal economic opportunities. Our banking system was one where most banks were community banks making small asset-based loans (generally under $500,000) within their local area. These loans created small businesses, the mom and pop stores that employed millions of people, and supported a strong nation supported by financially strong smaller communities.

The key being that these loans were on assets, and it created a world of economic opportunities by providing funds for new startups, based on assets and the credit-worthiness of the individual.

But today, our "financial system" consists of a few big banks making only cash-flow loans of multi-million and multi-billion dollars in a few select markets. But loans based only on "an existing cash flow" is economic nonsense. The whole idea of economic opportunity is on the acquiring of assets.

Crooks eager to get their hands on your cash are leading us to economic ruin.

Our politicians talk about "creating jobs" – when they

destroyed the very economy, the free enterprise system, that created them. If it wasn't so pitiful, it would be laughable.

State Capitalism is a system of economic plunder – a socialistic partnership between big business and big government.

While there is no doubt that large firms need large loans, making only large loans is financial stupidity. For instance, plankton survived as the dinosaurs died off, and Dollar Stores have more walk-in customers than General Motors . . . and are more profitable.

A financial genius should know that a ten mile an hour breeze is nice but a tornado is dangerous. As our recent history proves, a hundred million small businesses build a better, stronger, and safer economy than 5,000 huge conglomerates - and provide for a hell'ova' lot more service.

Reality demonstrates that if one small business dies it doesn't make a blip on the economy, but when an Enron, Lehman Bros, General Motors, or some other behemoth falls, the stock market goes into a panic mode.

And our political and financial wonders can't see *their stupidity* at work?

Professional liars and talking heads tell us that our entrepreneurial "Capitalistic" spirit will get us out of this mess. But there is a world of difference between the capitalism of private enterprise and the corrupted "capitalism" of State promoted, sponsored, and regulated business partnerships.

To understand our current situation, start by ignoring all the Happy Talk noise coming from the economic experts, especially from media talking heads and elected officials.

Their solution is more government, bigger deals, borrow more money, add to the debt, print more money, and lie. It is a recipe for failure.
No. It's more than that ...

It is a recipe for disaster.

Most of our financial and political leaders should be in jail. But we keep re-electing the same philosophy to office...a perfect wrong action for correcting our course. Long-term policy-makers live in a campaign mode, with many, many side excursions into feathering their own nests, which is conducive to more collective government.

The failure of every political office-holder or candidate, bank CEOs, stock peddlers, conglomerate chiefs, and know-nothing economists, to understand – or acknowledge – how we destroyed our economic foundation, and what we must do to rebuild it, shows the depth of our economic stupidity.

There is no one giving serious consideration as to how we actually got in this mess. We are concentrating on the symptoms, not the cause. Nor do our politicians and talking heads know how to get us out of it.

As long as we, the voters, swallow the hokum of State Capitalism, things will continue to get worse . . .

Wake up and smell your future.

2 LIES! LIES! LIES!
The Foundation of Government

Those in government want those of us who are not in government to believe that government is perfect.

They want us believing it can do no wrong and, if it does, by chance, do wrong, it is because of some who do not appreciate what government is doing for them.

And "government will correct" it is the song sung by those telling us lies.

Government expands on systemic lies and fraud. If you keep it simple and follow the money, fraud is the foundation of our US economy. Government, despite what you might want to believe, runs the US economy. And that is why, like government, our entire financial system is doing only one thing well: Lie.

Start with the government promise of job creation and economic opportunity. Over the past three decades, government has killed more jobs than it created, and has denied economic opportunities to all but a select class of its partners.

Yet, politicians continuously spout off about "creating jobs" and "the economy."

First, Congress has farmed out its authority and responsibility to

oversee all money bills, and the economy, turning these things over to the Federal Reserve Board.

Government allows the men and women at the Fed to protect and carry out their one common goal: To protect the interests of big banks and their financial partners, such as Goldman Sachs, Morgan Stanley, AIG, etc.

Next, when our government, which is to protect us from enemies from without and within, supposedly, allowed banks to switch from an economy based on lending on assets to "cash flow" loans, opportunities for private enterprise died.

We killed it by force-feeding the economy the new State Capitalism, the partnership between big business and big government (the new socialism). Loans for modest, honest, reliable mom and pop endeavors, and other small businesses that created most of the nation's jobs, disappeared. They were replaced by multi-billion-dollar opportunities for large corporations, the nation's conglomerates and monopolies, to engage in mergers, buyouts, and takeovers.

As small businesses vanished, millions of jobs also vanished, lost in the waste of State Capitalism. Employment opportunities are now limited to a tasteless fast-food industry and a few large box-stores or franchises.

We stopped making things.

American industry went offshore, using devaluation of our money against the values of other currencies to show a profit for the new internationals. They did this while our government subsidized them with tax dollars forced from American taxpayers at gunpoint.

As small businesses and jobs vanished, downtown areas in many large, medium and small towns turned into offices, vacant buildings, and antique junk places.

Small banks vanished. Between 1988 and 2010, we went from about 17,000 to just over 4,000 banks. All we have anymore are branch outlets of a few huge financial institutions selling stocks, bonds, insurance, and lending on any high-risk cash-flow speculative venture that will earn them a big fee. Deposits, seldom used for benefit in the local community where these outlets are located, are pipelined to distant, far-off headquarters.

Government told us that "bigger is better." It informed us that the changes in our banking system were to safeguard the integrity of the market place and to create new economic opportunities for all citizens. It was a lie.

The lie was to limit the number of banks, and block other banks from entering markets, to create a few giant financial institutions to serve America's 5,000 largest companies and corporations, and to establish increased fees to those able and willing to pay them.

The lie gave a few fast money boys vast opportunities to come up with new ways to create cash-flow markets (beyond the billions of dollars generated from illegal drugs), such as hedge funds and derivatives.

The banks' influence over these markets had costly implications for the economy; especially, for small businesses, average families, and individuals.

We had stock traders and bankers and other financial experts dazzling the economic world with their ability to make money. Well, at least on paper. Based on lies of ever-increasing profits and profitable returns, large and small investors poured money into a rapidly rising stock market. Government killed other worthwhile opportunities for investment, leaving only the stock markets.

Where else can a small investor put what little money they have into something that offers a return on their money, except the stock markets?

Beginning in the mid-1980s, new bankruptcies were being reported almost monthly of major large firms that were failing. But few investors ever asked publicly, "how is it possible for these firms to lose all that money and the market continue to rise?"

It was – and is – an unnatural economic world built on lies.

Beginning in March of 2009, the Feds have used the taxpayers' $3.3 trillion in bailout cash to benefit a few financial giants. Goldman Sachs helped itself 212 times - roughly every business day - during the next 12-month period, all the while telling the world that it needed no bailout. Other financial institutions that actually did not need the taxpayer's money also helped themselves.

Most everything from government is a lie:

We're told that Social Security and Medicare are leading us to bankruptcy. But seldom are loan guarantees, grants and subsidies for monopolies and conglomerates, spending billions in creating jobs overseas, ever mentioned.

Never is the "pork barrel" empty.

We're told that each of us lives only at the expense of someone else.

Government encouraged, enhanced the financial expert's lie that the stock market would make you rich: All you had to do was invest in some mutual fund of the month they peddle – and hold on to the shares for a long time.

At least, long enough to generate more "management fees".

The "bigger is better" nonsense – that government and a few conglomerates could build a better economic system – was and is a lie.

Another lie was that *if* State Capitalism did not make people rich, government would provide everyone "a safety net" that they were entitled to...

There was the lie that faith in government is all that is required to provide a value for money. There was the lie that government debt did not matter, as it was debt owed to ourselves. Well, now we are $19.3 trillion in debt and the bill is in the mail.

There is the lie that *the intent* of a government program is more important than results.

There is the lie that financial speculators are "too big to fail."

There is the Big Lie that pumping trillions of dollars into the economy will lead to economic opportunities and prosperity.

Now, our government has us headed toward federal government bankruptcy, and the lies continue: Don't worry. Stay the course. Government will take care of you. Trust us.

Lies. And more lies.

Beginning in the late 1970's, the Feds used trillions and trillions of the taxpayer's money to benefit a few financial giants. Yet, we're told that the government needs more money to reduce the federal deficit; that not raising taxes is a "cost" to the government; and that government cannot find a place or a way to reduce spending. (But taxes are a "cost" to taxpayers, not the government -)

No one is saying that the more money government takes, the more money it will spend.

No one is saying that places to reduce spending are the programs like the $3.3 trillion to financial institutions; and the trillions shelled out in subsidies to a few large conglomerates and a few favored "green" industries and alternative fuels.

No one is saying that we can't afford government taking care of us.

No one is saying stop the lies.

3 POLITICAL FOLLY

Political philosophy that leads to "folly, vice, and madness, without intuition or restraint" is the hallmark of progressive thought.

American liberals fail to understand that an effort to be "neat, with it, cool, hip, groovy, a dish, hot, etc.," never makes up for being bone-deep stupid or ignorant.

If you're working at being *"hip and with it"* you ain't . . .

Think President Obama and the Washington line-up of self-proclaimed or voting-record socialists, regardless of party.

Edmund Burke described these gabby wonders when he wrote, "Those who know what virtuous liberty is, cannot bear to see it disgraced by incapable heads, on account of their having high-sounding words in their mouths."

That is the divide.

Today, millions of us admire President Obama's gift of gab while intensely disliking and fearing his ideas for a socialist America. And Congress is full of others blessed with high-sounding socialistic words echoing from incapable heads.

Since 1960, Americans have been wandering the wilderness of irrational "social" economics as seen by the nation's progressives. The theories expounded were thoroughly debunked by noted economist Ludwig von Mises in 1951. But too few listened . . .

America has changed from the United State's prosperity and freedom of the decades when parents could raise their kids to understand and abide by recognized and understood values; and anyone could build an automobile the way they saw fit, log the forests, mine the lands, raise and sell animals, etc., to today's USA that is *$19 Trillion* in debt.

What happened?

A growth in "central planning" (a form of rigging the system) is the culprit. No matter which politically well-connected group does it, rigging the system violates our core principle of equal protection under the law.

Under "central planning" for every imaginable program or cause, politicians have eliminated thousands of community banks and replaced them with a few humongous national financial institutions.

They created "special groups" of special people for preferred treatment; stacked the stock markets; encouraged formation of monopolies and conglomerates; and took control of education in local schools and universities.

In short, those we elected to public office destroyed fundamental concepts of right and wrong, and have taken social and economic control of our lives.

Talk of "non-partisanship" and the old saw *that politics can be removed from politics* was designed to disarm all of us into not thoroughly thinking through the phony *politics of scarcity*, which passes for "science" and "planning" nowadays.

If you can designate something as facing "scarcity", America's low-information, emotional, non-thinking – but hip and with it – voter will allow you to *protect* and *conserve* (or *control)* it, while uttering something about "good policy".

But central control cannot co-exist with private property. Control equals ownership. If you can control it, does it matter who owns it?

Karl Marx, through his seductive and now proven lie that central control increases total production, is how communism abolished private property; a belief now favored by only stupid utopians.

But it's not complicated. Central control abolishes private property – it "communizes" property. The system becomes a game. This rigging of the system destroys opportunity for shared prosperity, and spells economic disaster for everyone but a favored few elites.

The philosophy of America's exceptionalism through the protection of life, liberty and property of the individual is far more important than vague references to "good policy".

Our Founders feared a powerful central government. One was trying to imprison or kill them, and was destroying their livelihoods.

They disfavored monopolies, favored equal treatment under the law, and considered "Every man has his price" a degraded model.

We are in the mess we're in because top-down central planning pushed a progressive program of State Capitalism, a partnership between Big Business and Big Government (America's new version of socialism).

For over a half-century, our ignorance let us listen to false prophets.

How dumb are we?

Central planning leads to control. But strange new words describing old socialist ideas are out of Pandora's box and floating around freely.

Once, both major political parties had a cautious sense that civil society *is* fragile, and that it should only be altered carefully. There was an insistence that with rights come responsibilities. There was an understanding that each individual was charged with making the most of his or her liberty.

That sense that guided the best elements of both major parties for so long has been lurching into something different over recent years — a creep toward the socialist's embrace of ignorance and fear, packaged in the American "Progressivism" pushed today by self-proclaimed elites.

This is why today, despite all the pressure to do so,

there are NO conservatives embracing "Washington Politicians".

Or a philosophy of socialism.

Policy is the implementation of a philosophy.

Philosophy is a set of principles to live by.

And progressive thought reflects the regurgitated policies that lead to the *"folly, vice, and madness, without intuition or restraint"* of socialism.

You cannot be *with it* by embracing the enslavement and misery of collectivist socialism.

That is not *hip* . . .
. . . nor intelligent.

4 WAVING BYE-BYE

Now that the car companies, financial institutions and other "too big to fail" conglomerates have failed, because of the Big Business and Big Government partnership that is State Capitalism, you can wave bye-bye to the middle class in America.

This isn't some fantasy: It's the handwriting on the wall. The writing was done over decades as America abandoned our system of private enterprise. Instead of worry that middle-class incomes had stopped growing, we were listening to the assumptions of "feel good" socialism and "compassionate" liberalism.

We were – and are – listening to false prophets.

Now, middle class incomes are vanishing, and soon all that will be left is a small privileged class and a mass of us caught in economic slavery.

The sociopolitical implications are terrifying.

As we are waving good-bye to the economy, we should remember that we brought it on ourselves.

We elected the weak-minded because they were one of us. Like us, the voter, they talked the big talk, but couldn't walk a straight line or maintain a straight thought.

Today, the same failed economic and political prophets are promising new technologies that will deliver hydrogen-power, hybrid-electrical-power, solar-power, wind-power, fusion-power, green power, people-power, etc., at unbelievable low prices! And they will deliver it to every home, business and what-all in existence – *the first thing tomorrow morning!*

Basically, we're being conned into believing "perpetual motion" works.

First of all, under our system of State Capitalism system the bulk of taxes for research into all these promised new energy sources is going to the monopoly currently over-charging us for hydrocarbon fuel. Every nut but a politician knows that an alternative energy source will only hit the market when the profit from it equals or surpasses the profit now being ripped from oil and gas.

As long as the monopolies now in control of energy are in control of developing new sources of energy . . . we ain't gonna' get one new source of energy until it's as profitable as the old energy!

The partners in State Capitalism want us to dream and fantasize about low-cost new-energy: The last thing they want is a thinking consumer and thinking voter. Let's face it, our stupidity is in their best interest.

And as long as the top rated TV shows are inane fluff, such as American Idol, Secret Life of a Teenage Mother, Dancing with the Stars, Survival, etc., and major networks waste hours of airtime on the death of some teen idol no-class, no-taste, druggie pervert, we're not likely to get over our stupidity.

As long as we're taking political and cultural advice from idiots who have somehow managed to make it onto the big screen without a brain, we're not likely to get over our stupidity.

As long as we think sixteen year olds who can't carry a tune without it coming thru their nose or try to play a guitar while screaming and bellowing is "talent", we're not going to get over our stupidity. And just as long as recording companies keep pushing simple music for simple people, we're not going to get over our stupidity.

As long as we fail to recognize that playing an "X-box game" is a damn poor, pitiful excuse for not reading, we're not going to get over our stupidity.

As long as we think tattoos and body-piercings are a good fashion statement, we're not going to get over our stupidity.

Even more importantly, as long as we vote the way we have for the same politician, or the same kind of politicians we have, we're not going to get over our stupidity.

Assuming some Americans *could* rise above our mass stupidity, would there be enough of us to change the way we're going . . . ?

We obviously require a drastic revision of our current collective self-image, of what we aspire to be and who we are.

But will we do it, or continue to venture off into silly mind-numbing nothings and continue to be sold grandiose schemes and accept lectures of what is politically correct from those we wouldn't invite into our homes?

We are approaching a point of not will we do it, but can we do it?

If America is to have any future of freedom and economic choice at all, we must –

But back to the energy question: Notice, there is also some talk about "natural gas" as a fuel? The reason why we don't hear more of it, is that it too, is controlled by the hydrocarbon boys. Sure, it's plentiful: Enough here at home to fuel all today's energy needs for centuries. So, why aren't we using it?

Current profits are why.

There's so much natural gas and it's so easy to get to, compared to places we're now drilling for oil, it would be almost impossible to keep the independents out. Monopolies eliminated thousands of independent oil companies during the "oil shortages of the 70's". Now, they make sure that no door is opened.

28

An open door to independent endeavors would mean competition, which might hurt those profits.

Monopolies can keep high prices at the pump – and will, as long as we restrict competition.

But it's very hard to keep good news down. Therefore, the State Capitalistic partners must crank up the propaganda outlets and start spinning out make-believe reasons:

Because of the lack of the necessary delivery system to get it to the pumps.

Because of the logistics involved in replacing the old gas stations.

Because of the technical problems of the vehicle manufacturers (but don't think about the time and expense we're wasting on hybrids and electric cars?)

And more *"Because...Because...Because..."*

We have the "Hope and Change" in the nationalization of GM solving our all our automobile problems. Forget that the odds are pretty high that any new products the geniuses now in charge come up with will fail against the established competition.

We have "Hope and Change" now owning most of the financial institutions: The same bunch that managed our nation's finances so well they've given us a $19.1 trillion - and growing - debt.

And we have the same bunch in both political parties pleading, "Don't blame us!"

We have "Hope and Change" doing to our nation what it's done to the middle class.

We have "Hope and Change" replacing the real-world reality.

We have the embodiment of "Hope and Change" in the brave new world of State Capitalism.

But, we need more than "Hope and Change" slogans.

Voters need to remember Street's Absolute Rules of Government:

"Government creates government."

"If you use government, government will use you."

"The bigger the government, the less government is concerned about you."

"The smarter you are the less government you need."

Street's Absolute Rule of Consumerism can also apply to government: *"The more people who want it, the less you need it."*

5 SHOPPING

If you are a shopper, and we all are at sometime, get ready: The government is getting ready to screw you. Again.

For years, when new models or new styles started to arrive in stores and showrooms most retailers would start trying to sell off any inventory of older merchandise to make room for the newer ones. They generally put the older stuff on sale, marking the price down to hopefully clear out the inventory.

Many smart shoppers would wait or try and time their purchases to take advantage of these lower prices, which sometimes offered significant savings.

This was an economic system dependent upon a variety of manufacturers, wholesalers, retailers and smart shoppers.

It was a system with competitiveness as the key ingredient.

But this system is approaching its last days; destroyed by State Capitalism, the partnership of Big Business and Big Government.

For the last two decades, our recent economic system of State Capitalism has deliberately killed economic opportunity for small business startups by eliminating availability of funds for the assets needed to make things. It was a way to eliminate competition. And it has worked all across the economic landscape.

Before explaining what is in store for shoppers, we should explain why it is coming:

First, government allowed the artificial "gas shortages" of the mid-1970's, by a few Big Oil companies, and government allows the high gas prices of today. Government allowed Big Oil to eliminate the smaller independent oil producers and the thousands of independent distributors and the more thousands and thousands of independent service stations.

It was this competition within the oil industry which created a relatively free-market - and a relatively reasonable - price of energy.

Government, the Department of Energy, allowed the companies (screaming about shortages that did not exist and that has never existed) to eliminate their competition.

Today, the three or four energy conglomerates that remain control the price consumers pay at the pump – while they and their friends make billions speculating on the price of the oil and gas they control.

32

And because of financial campaign favors and key jobs for relatives, Congress can't seem to figure out the problem . . .

Next, the Federal Reserve, controlled by Wall Street bankers who convinced Congress, with timely applied campaign contributions and financial favors, to destroy the nation's banking system by lifting barriers on fiduciary standards, thereby creating "financial institutions" that could engage in every kind of financial shenanigan.

Since 1980, under State Capitalism, the total number of banks in America dropped from over 15,000 to less than 4,500 today. Small community-owned banks have virtually disappeared, swallowed by the big banks.

The Feds replaced asset-based loans, the backbone for creating economic activity, with a policy of "cash-flow" loans only, which are great for laundering drug money and collecting big fees for doing so, but offer nothing as a means for creating small economic opportunities. Congress polished off all this stupidity by allowing the adjustable interest rate, which only socializes the bad judgment of the "financial experts". And in our State Capitalism stupidity, voters allow Congress to guarantee the multi-millions and billions in bad loans made by these "experts" - and the money keeps disappearing and no one knows where it has gone - not even Congress, which knows everything.

Now, we are back to the past in retail circles under our system of State Capitalism, which is a smelly something called a Unilateral Pricing Policy (UPP).

For years, manufacturers have used a Minimum Advertised Pricing (MAP) policy: It is a pricing deal on or with those products for which a manufacturer provides advertising funds to a retailer to advertise their product or products. Acceptance of the co-op advertising funds means the retailer must not price a product below a set minimum price. (This is the reason why you often must actually go through an online retailer's checkout cart before a price becomes visible.) But if a retailer is willing to lose the co-op advertising funds, they can sell the product for whatever price they want or can get for it.

Under MAP, the retailer has a choice.

But with a Unilateral Pricing Policy (UPP), a manufacturer can cut off the retailer's products if the retailer advertises or sells the product for less than the predetermined minimum price as set by the manufacturer. This leaves little wiggle room for retail dealers to advertise or sell the products for less than the predetermined minimum price set by the manufacturer. It leaves no wiggle room for retailers to out-discount their competitors.

In practice, UPP actually penalizes retailers for selling a product below the manufacturer's preset price. Under UPP, the retailer has no choice.

And this is not good for the retailer, nor the shopper. It is not good for the economy. It is not good for choice. The manufacturer essentially controls the retailer's business.

How is this good for economic freedom?

Manufacturers say the move to UPP is a way to cut the number of dealers it sells to directly, and even restrict the sale of its products via third-party resellers. This, of course, is a bunch of nonsense: They see it as the way to maximize profit (or as they call it, pricing stability for their products in the market). Regardless of what they may claim, UPP means that the shopper will pay more rigorous, higher prices.

What all this means for those of us looking for bargains is that prices on products from fewer and fewer manufacturers will soon be "fixed," much the way products from Apple and Bose tend to be sold at the same prices, regardless of the retailer.

Unilateral Pricing Policy (UPP) can only exist under State Capitalism, whereby economic opportunity, which creates competitiveness among manufacturers, is not allowed.

Under our State Capitalism drift, government is forcing shoppers - consumers - to guarantee a few, selected manufacturers a profit to go along with the guarantees made to Big Oil and other Big Companies by our Big Government.

Of course, as economic opportunities continue their downward spiral, it will not be long before our worries will change from shopping to survival.

Reducing economic opportunities to gain more control over the lives of citizens is the goal of State Capitalism. It is far easier to control a few big monopolies or conglomerates than it is 320-million-plus Americans.

Perhaps, more of us should have spent more time thinking about the Idea of America than shopping for trinkets.

6 "THERE'S NO BUSINESS LIKE . . ."

Those of us who are not in show business are bombarded with publicity from talent agencies and promoters ballyhooing the imagination and creative ability of some artist or entertainer or a wonderfully entertaining event.

Culture.

Hotdog!

For some time now, government has subsidized artists and entertainers in all kinds, types, and styles of "culturally diverse" venues. And government tells us how important it is to provide funds to encourage and support the world of art and creative efforts.

And over 99% of the tax dollars end up being wasted on pure crap.

Take a moment and think about that...

Not every song, every movie, every play, every painting or drawing or sketch, or every written page, is worthy of seeing the light of day. Creativity strikes out more often than a big league baseball pitcher at bat.

Government subsidies reward too many people with mediocre or no talent over those with vastly superior talent or greater abilities.

This is because government rewards individuals with an immense drive to secure funds over those driven to obey the demands of talent or ability. Government subsidizes its' work similar to the way that George Burns once described acting: *"Acting is all about honesty. If you can fake that, you've got it made."*

In America today, if you can dot the government "I" and cross the government "T", you can get someone else's money.

You may be incapable of thinking, unskilled in singing or acting (or both), lack knowledge of composition, don't know one end of the brush from the other, blow more hot air than glass, and still be rewarded with tax dollars.

All it takes is a desire for it and the drive to have some bureaucracy hand it to you.

This is not saying that all artists and/or entertainers or entertainment venues receiving a government hand-out are without talent or ability or are worthwhile; just most. But while they may be lacking, they likely are more intelligent than some with a greater ability or more talent: They know how to get money they didn't work for and that they don't deserve.

But just because an individual was blessed with some great talent doesn't mean they were necessarily blessed with a great intellect.

Sometimes, one interferes with the other. Often, there seems to be trade-off, a penalty for the gift of a great ability or talent.

The number of individuals who were given a wonderful talent or ability in an art or entertainment field and who were short-changed in common sense (or a lack in the ability to think) amazes us. Before the movies and TV, only pigs produced ham and chickens laid eggs. Now, we have talented hams laying rotten eggs while grunting and crowing about the need for more big government.

Mistaking a talent for intelligence, some of these dim-witted creatures end up braying about a need they perceive that requires being controlled by a centralized government. But at the same time, they are people who demand recognition as "creative, intelligent, and fiercely independent" individuals. And they are too damn dumb to see their intellectual dishonesty.

They rush to the microphone or before the camera to tell us poor slobs "out in TV land" of their wonderful feelings for what needs to be done and how they feel the government should be doing whatever their feelings want done ... and the brain-damaged among us hang on to their every worthless, brainless word – and *feel just like they do . . .*

These artists and entertainers are going to love feeling the results of the big government they advocate.

Think how the artist will love being told to paint only Aryan blondes with large strong breasts. The movie folks can rejoice when informed that the only roles available are for demonstrating and showing the products of the government production lines. Oh, how joyfully the composers and singers will sound the notes of only those songs praising the glories of the state which they are allowed to record. And how happy will be all the writers and the publishers when they are restricted to booklets of indoctrination and instruction and printing the changing, and always growing, lists of penalties for non-approved behavior.

So, take another moment and think about that. . .

. . . and how these artists and entertainers are helping to speed us all to that Happy Day.

What will their feelings be then, while waiting for the knock on the door?

7 PATHS TO ECONOMIC COLLAPSE

In time's scheme, not too long ago, back in 1972, for every dollar in circulation, there was a coinciding amount of gold to back it up; a gold standard.

A banker or even a group of bankers or another country had a hard time manipulating the value of gold.

Actually, for centuries, all the major money systems of the world were anchored by gold. All countries based their currencies (paper money) on gold. When one traded with another, both were certain that gold was backing their currency, and that the currency had value.

Politicians began to tear down this system during the prosperity of the nineteenth century. During WWI, Britain and France borrowed too much, and then they couldn't pay it back because they didn't have enough gold to pay the expenses.

During the 1930's, FDR made it illegal for individual citizens to own gold. Even so, some parts of a gold-backed system lingered on throughout the twentieth century (though not perfectly); and the last stage of this system lasted until 1971.

Roosevelt swung open government purse-strings during the Great Depression. Following WWII, we had Kennedy's New Frontier, Johnson's Great Society and the Vietnam War, and these experiments in social engineering were extremely expensive.

And we started electing to office politicians who found the best way to keep getting re-elected was to give the masses guns and butter.

Conservatives warned that the nation couldn't afford deficit spending, that we couldn't afford both guns and butter, that it won't work, we can't afford it.

The Democrats, now predominately made up of liberals, and led by Johnson, said, "Oh, yes we can; we're a big rich country, we can afford both guns and butter." Well, they couldn't without raising taxes. But they didn't want to raise taxes because then they wouldn't be re-elected. And what resulted was a run on our money.

Other countries, especially the French, led by Charles de Gaulle, noticing that the dollar was weakening told then-President Nixon they wanted to exchange the dollars they were holding for gold.

Nixon examined the situation and realized that if we allowed the exchange, the United States would not have much gold left. So, he decided to close the gold window. That was August 15, 1971, and since then, no foreign government could trade dollars for gold.

At that time, on the world stage, an ounce of gold was worth around 35 U.S. Dollars.

Thanks to social engineering and the bad habit of re-electing the same crooked politicians to office, over and over and over, our dollar now is only as good as our faith in our government.

With the value of a dollar a thing of the past, without some standard of value, when the Fed determines that the economy needs a stimulus, they can print more money or lower interest rates. Borrowing becomes easier when they do, and more money flows into the economy. This is known as opening the Fed window, and the result is an increase in the money supply.

This creates a paradox:

As the money supply increases, weakening the dollar even more, consumers (most of whom are desperate to spend their money somewhere, as they have been told to do) tend to feel wealthier as more money changes hands as they buy goods and services. This puts a chain of events into motion.

Businesses seeing increased sales order more materials and increase production. This, in turn, increases the demand for labor and goods.

Next, the prices of stocks rise and firms issue equity and debt. (When investors purchase stock they're buying debt of the company issuing the shares.) As the money supply continues to expand, the prices for goods and services increase.

As the public accepts inflation, the nation's lenders insist on higher interest rates to offset the expected decline in purchasing power over the life of their loans. This rewards the Con Artists and Crap Shooters who create strange and new ways to bilk investors in an expanding economy - and collect big fees while doing so.

When inflation is rising, the dollar loses its value, and the Fed raises interest rates, which means borrowing becomes more expensive. But under present lending policies, money flows out of the economy and into the hands of the lenders and the fee-based speculators. And the circulation of money fails to reach all segments of the economy.

Then, when overall economic activity slows, economic forecasters start raving about the declining rate of economic growth. And about the resulting disinflation (reduced inflation) or deflation (falling prices).

In a worst-case scenario, which the most optimistic among us claim we're now in, the economy can become both stagnant and inflation simultaneously, a situation called "stagflation".

The Fed is then faced with an extremely difficult choice, because it cannot raise interest rates and lower them at the same time. It must choose either to stimulate the economy or to fight inflation.

For instance, what happened in the United States in the late 1970's, proved to be a very difficult time for the country.

The forces of inflation had been picking up steam throughout the 1970's, and the prices of just about everything were hitting record highs (until the record highs of today). History shows the Federal Reserve was part of the problem. They let the money supply get out of control because of guarantees made by government leaders.

Inflation had reached a crisis point, with the Fed's key interest rate rising to over 12-percent.

By the late 1970's, consumers saw interest rates topping 25%.

The rapidity of inflation increases during this decade gave birth to the Adjustable Interest Rate, which socializes the bad judgment of a banker. Bankers, who are supposed to be the experts on money, and control the flow of money, need to be held accountable for their decisions. Before the Adjustable Interest Rate there were seldom any wild, wide-swings in the economy. Bankers couldn't afford to mess up big time. Now, they could, can, and do.

The Adjustable Interest Rate was to assure banks a profit under the new policy of having a desired inflationary rate, which the Fed had set at 1% to 3% annually.

This was quickly followed by the Adjustable Rate Mortgage. And only a politician would fail to see where this has gotten us.

Inflation, back in the 1960s, exploded under Kennedy and Johnson: Government was spending so much on domestic policies that little money was available for foreign loans.

So, a deal was struck between the political leaders in both parties (who were increasingly liberal) and the Fed, agreeing that they would loan money to foreign countries: The larger member banks of the Fed would make the loans to the foreign countries (at the highest possible interest rate), and the United States government (read taxpayers) would guarantee the loans.

It was a win-win deal for the bankers and the government.

Supposedly, the leaders of those countries receiving loans would be friendly to the U. S. government who was guaranteeing the loans. The banks providing the money would be raking in high interest rates. The only possible losers would be the unsuspecting taxpayer.

And we were the losers.

The nation's bankers were making huge loans to foreign governments at previously unheard of rates of interest. In terms of paperwork, these big loans were no more expensive to make than small loans, the interest rates were higher, and the loans were backed by a government guarantee.

It didn't take long before bankers wanted those 12 and 15-percent interest rates on loans here at home, too, which led to the high interest rates of the late 70's/early 80's.

When foreign countries could not or would not pay back the loans or even the high interest payments, the American bankers demanded payment under the guarantee. But this was politically impossible.

So, naturally, another deal was struck between the Fed and key politicians, which led to the bailout of the nation's banks in the mid-80s. This cost taxpayers billions, saw a reduction in the total number of banks (from over 17,000 to now less than 4,700), eliminated asset-lending in favor of only "cash-flow" loans, and allowed rapid inflation.

All of this, as we warned at the time, was creating State Capitalism, a partnership between Big Business and Big Government.

We warned, fruitlessly, that State Capitalism has nothing to do with a private economic system, but much to do with socialism.

We repeatedly warned that the results of State Capitalism would wipe out economic opportunity for millions of Americans, resulting in unacceptable economic performance, inflation, and a collapse of our financial system.

But few listened!

America does not have a hereditary ruling class, but we have created State Capitalism, a system that gives handed-down wealth to plenty of people who love weakening the system and feeding greedily at the trough. State Capitalism has created and is creating special favors and special privileges for a growing group of "our kind of people".

When we traded Private Enterprise for State Capitalism we created today's problems!

When we traded asset-based lending for "cash-flow" loans we increased the problems!

When we socialized the bad judgment of bankers with the Adjustable Interest Rate we opened the door to all kinds of wrong-doing!

There is little hope for individual economic opportunity in our economy anymore; all we have is the grandstanding and chicanery of Big Business and Big Government. Many knowing that something is wrong, but not knowing what, bought into the recent "hope and change" nonsense of the far left - which has only increased things that were wrong.

And still others support State Capitalism because of the money government hands them!

The only national leadership we have anymore now utters weaseling criticisms against those who warn about way too much government and way too little accountability.

Conservatives, who should know better, talk of our "capitalistic" society or "capitalism"; a term made infamous by Karl Marx. They, like most of us, have forgotten the Private Enterprise System, the bedrock of our economic foundation.

Today, instead of moving back onto the firmer ground of a private enterprise system, the greatest economic system the world has ever known, we're falling ever deeper into the crevices of State Capitalism.

Those in Congress who made it all possible during their long years in office, were demanded to give more to those who gave to them, created more inflation by plunging the nation into a morass of debt and economic slavery.

Nationalization of firms "too big to fail" is socialism.

How can any rational mind think that the ones who got us into this mess can get us out?

Think of the Federal Reserve Board as the bank of banks, which it really is, but acts like a government central bank, which it isn't. It is a private bank for the nation's big bankers. And it is the primary force in determining our nation's money supply.

Unfortunately, the nine individuals who make up the Fed's governing committee are primarily "experts from the financial world"; and their private goals are in conflict with the nation's public goals as set forth in our Constitution.

Congress has given this dysfunctional Fed the job of being the gatekeeper of the U.S. economy. A gatekeeper is, of course, the fellow who sits on a rail above it all and lets the bull out.

And our economy is collapsing because, instead of thinking, we listen to the bellowing...

8 CHOICES

Civilization started with the discovery of fire.

But if government control the progressive-regressives and their emotionally-deranged supporters have their way, our civilization will be better without fire (as fire kills more people annually than guns).

Gun control is the same ancient institutional thinking that promoted societal controls that gave rise to eunuchs, chastity belts, harems, and today's *modern nations* stoning to death unfaithful wives and curious daughters.

Progressives talk of "reasonable" restrictions on the Constitution, on the Bill of Rights. They make more or other restrictions sound so reasonable (to sick and uninformed minds), especially when it comes to gun control – and government help.

But if government control was part of *nature's game plan*, killer bees and fire-ants, scorpions, rattlesnakes, rabid animals, and worlds of other stinging and biting and killing - including those done by man - wouldn't be part of it.

Most of government is unnatural.

Voters should never forget that the states formed the federal government and, in doing so, tried their very best to protect themselves from a centralized, all-powerful form of government – like the one they were fighting in order to secure their freedom.

This is why we have a Bill of Rights. These men were not about to again give any form of government control over their lives, not ever.

They worked and argued and discussed and together decided that they would tie the hands of the government they were forming so that it could never become the kind of government that was trying hard to kill each and every one of them. Any idiot who doesn't understand this basic fact, who believes "reasonable" changes to the Constitution (on which the signing of their name was a death warrant), should never be elected to office.

It is likely they would be too dumb to know what "reasonable" is . . .

And there must be some common-sense standard – as set forth in the Constitution.

Tomorrow is yesterday's dream.

Is today that "yesterday's dream" that our nation's founders wanted?

Is today our dream? If so, haven't we sold America's tomorrow short?

The Declaration of Independence proclaimed liberty not only for America, but, as Lincoln said, *"...to the world"*.

The Constitution is an inspired set of profound principles – not theories of questionable issues swayed by some questionable current of popular opinion – as found in the Bill of Rights: the fundamental guarantee of the principle of Freedom from Government.

If we, as a nation, wish to change or do away with some principle enumerated in the Bill of Rights (and in our Constitution), there is a way – *a principle* – on how to do it.

If we, as a nation, are to remain free, changes must be accomplished according to the principle available in the Constitution.

But there are those who seek to change it or destroy it, not by principle, but by ignoring the principles or composing some "Executive Order", "Official Directive" or "Agency Policy".

Politicians, especially those with progressive stripes, love poor people or they would not have created so many of them (as Mark Twain observed about God and flies).

And pitiful cries of annoyance and denial, and charges of uncaring and no feeling for the unfortunate, won't change the fact that government does its damnedest to create poor people.

America's growing welfare roll with its' expanding number of unemployed and under-employed, and the continuing plunge in family income, are all the results of increased socialism sponsored by progressives and endorsed by the stupid.

First, cooperating politicians killed the Private Enterprise System – the greatest economic system the world has ever known – and replaced it with State Capitalism, a partnership between Big Business and Big Government. This they did by simply (a) replacing banks with financial institutions "too big to fail" and (2) socializing the bad judgment of financial experts with "adjustable interest rates" on loans (which the government guarantees).

Adding insult, they declared that assets were worthless, as the only available loans would be based on *existing* cash-flow.

You can be in debt over your head and have no real assets (except for a bag of "nose candy" or some other funny stuff that can be smoked, sniffed, swallowed or injected), but as long as you can claim a cash-flow somewhere, and you're willing to pay a Big Fee, securing a loan is no problem. Of course, you may have to *give someone a part of your enterprise* for it.

You can get a *BIG* loan on a cash-flow, which can quickly vanish into thin air, as a lot of crooks such as Corrizone, Madoff, and others have proven. But you cannot secure a loan on assets needed to create a new business; assets such as land, building, equipment, fixtures, inventory, etc. All of which are forms of savings.

They are also assets needed to make things, and this making and selling of things create jobs.

Progressives, who know that, basically, socialism is the control of the means and methods of production, also know that the only way to do control is by a centralized form of government.

And a rapidly expanding centralized government is what we – the voters – have allowed the progressives to create.

In their insane rush to socialism, progressives killed independent, small business opportunities by the restrictions on asset-based lending. This policy had the additional consequence of wiping out the downtown areas of thousands of small towns and communities. The few local remaining banks are not allowed to make loans on those private assets that also build communities.

Today, progressives lie about the subsidizing of large industries and government-approved ventures, such as the waste of tax dollars going to fund the politically correct, but unsustainable, "green" industries.

And the stupidity rolls on in the "new, alternative energy" subsidies going to oil conglomerates and monopolies. (An oil giant will find an "alternative energy source" when the profit on it matches the current profits of oil and gas.)

Progressives fund "private" but government-sponsored (and participating) venture capital firms. This is socialistic-speak about "the way to increase the availability of growth capital for small businesses." And they tell us how these private-government firms "will stimulate job creation in (your city), by requiring the supported businesses hire at least 25% of their employees from poverty-levels or the unemployed..."

My, my, my . . .

"Government-sponsored venture capital initiatives" and the "public-private entrepreneurial job creators" are progressive programs supporting socialism.

Financial institutions, such as banks and insurance companies, that share in these programs' tax credits, equity, or profits are junior partners in our new American socialism.

They are enablers, capitalizing on capital; economic leeches sucking the lifeblood of every economic endeavor, especially new startups.

This is not job creation, nor is it economic progress.

Our present partnership between Big Business and Big Government, the system of State Capitalism, is evil – just as those who support and empower it are evil.

Might without responsibility or restraint is evil.

Progressives use these collaborators' desire for and acceptance of blood profits, to blind them into thinking they are some of the special few that deserve special treatment.

These collaborators are dissipating freedom; helping to stimulate the progressive's sick idea of economic socialism.

It is a way for government planners to consume large companies, small businesses, entrepreneurs, and new ideas. And they do it by and with progressive lies.

Progressives and other misguided and misinformed lovers of big government socialism will always be the catalyst advocating for a "developing and funding on-going programs for strategic investments" in federal, state, regional, and local infrastructure and public-private partnerships of all kinds, whether needed or not, worthwhile or not.

To these progressives, it is the concept, the idea, that is important – not the results.

Progressives always claim that (a) the need outpaces the funding and (b) programs must increase in size and power to maintain an acceptable level of service effectively over the long-term.

And there is always the plea for bipartisanship and meeting in the middle and cooperation: all rotten baloney designed to sell the gullible more socialism.

The sweet land of liberty is no more...

Both major parties share the blame. Dimocrats and bluenose Republicans, are malignant cancers eating away at the Constitution; both are morally responsible for corrupting principle after principle, dangerously weakening our Constitution.

This hostility to Constitutional mandates is a process approved by too many uniformed and ignorant voters, deluded and misled by the peculiar stench of mendacity and the stupidity displayed by those whom they vote into office.

But we shouldn't blame Congress: voters elected them.

Today, here is Congress – lolling in riches and luxury and mentally drugged with self-importance, seduced with blandishment by lobbyists and special interests, and degraded with ignorance and greed – their excuses for justification confounded by the extreme failure of their own causes and actions.

Those in Congress are assassins of freedom.

Is there no such thing as Treason?
    Are there no traitors?
    Are there no criminals?
    Are there no penalties?

Today, we are in an avalanche of socialism. It started slow, imperceptibly. But like the tide, it keeps coming, slowly building, pushing up, rising ever faster.

It's everywhere. A false promise in an idea, growing ever closer. Ever more powerful. Ever more dangerous.

It is going to swallow America. Soon.

You can see it. You may not know what it is or know all that comprises it, but you realize that chaos is inevitable –

You may regret it. You may hate the blissfully ignorant and the stupid who are responsible for the chaos that socialism is bringing, but you, deep down, know it is inevitable.

You wonder, you worry, about the choices you have, if any.

Can you afford to ignore it?

But how do you escape it?

We are swallowed by the realization of America's potential leaking away, of possibilities lost.

Spectators are all we are, spectators and sideline sitters, without a voice, without recourse to worthwhile action.

We were poisoned by our good intentions and our haste and our stupidity, all of it seasoned in the end by the greed and corruption of those we elected to serve us.

And by insider politics.

We are so far gone that we can no longer adapt to the new challenges of the new reality.

We live in a time when we want certainties, but face the loss of freedom and individuality.

It was – it is – our choice.

9 OUR MONEY HAS DONE GONE FUNNY....

....when we go to the grocery store, a dollar doesn't buy much anymore.

There's no such thing as a nickel candy bar or a ten-cent cigar, either. Everything from a paper-back book to an adult beverage comes in multiples of dollars. As Woody Allen observed, *"Man cannot live by bread alone; there must be an adult beverage sometime."*

When the only value of our money is only our faith in government, it's no wonder that our money "has gone funny".

Inflation has not only caught up with us, it has passed us and is still picking up speed.

The sad part of it is that it ain't funny when our money goes funny!

No, we're not going on a rant about decades of the Federal Reserve Board seeking 3% annual inflation or our politicians instituting policies for the benefit of stock market speculators, conglomerates, monopolies, and financial institutions.

Nor are we going to rant (here) on how those policies of the Fed and the politicians have reduced the value of our dollars every year, while penalizing those on fixed incomes and working men and women; and that are now destroying what was once the world's best economic system. We could. But, we won't.

The sad fact is, as Mel Waters sings, *"Everything's going up but my paycheck!"*

Fees charged by government are certainly going up.

Fees and prices in the private sector are certainly increasing, rapidly.

And those in government claim government needs more money.

Those in the private sector just keep raising prices because they can – there's no opportunity for new competition.

Nationwide, we've about killed off the goose that laid the golden egg.

When governmental units need more money, they eventually get around to raising taxes or going into debt.

The national boys and girls need trillions, our respective states need billions, our city needs millions, our schools need more millions, and our few Big Businesses want all they can gouge us for...

Taxpayers and citizens are being treated as sheep, sheered for their money.

When it comes to our money, even the numbers used can get funny.

And when it comes to our money, even the numbers used can "get funny."

Government tells us that they can take our money and stimulate the economy by keeping most of it for administrative purpose and spending what remains on "entitlements" or bailing out a few Big Businesses. Taxpayers who believe this ... this ... this ... *stuff* ... are funny, but it is not funny!

Funny how the same word can mean different things, isn't it?

What is not funny is that the vote of the average citizen provides no choice in what is happening – no options equal no freedom.

Economic and personal freedoms are ignored and down-graded, publicly.

Likely, the next generation or two will end up losing everything that America once represented. It is evident that some individuals have a more pronounced luxury of anticipation than others, and seek a hope for and a change to an European-styled Socialism.

At least, they're working hard for it.

They certainly are experts at ignoring private property rights and the freedom such rights inspire.

It seems most Americans love apathy.

Or, we are so intelligent and smart and good-looking, and beloved by all, that we only accept or want ideas from approved socialistic sources that tell us we're a great people –

- And great at romance.

Those looking for others who love freedom may get very lonely. And more financially broke.

Being human, despite some reports to the contrary, we realize that people hate criticism, and too many of us take it personally when it is meant professionally. We also know that some individuals never know the pain of contrition and afterthought; some lack the ability to look inside themselves and examine the unknown; and some have that something that stubbornly avoids progress or even change that leads to more freedom and self-responsibility.

It must be part of that "human nature" thing . . .

Anyway, after more than a half-century or so of shoveling trillions and trillions of dollars into government, we now are finding that we haven't gotten our money's worth. No problems have been solved, we are still not loved as a nation, and our freedom has disappeared.

Even free speech has been swallowed by political correctness and the air we breathe is taxed.

So, it's time for a little quid pro quo – a little what for what or something for something.

Or, is it too much to ask that government step up to the plate and deliver something of value in return for getting something of value?

If there is a way to get us back to stronger private property rights, a private enterprise system for local community banking based on asset lending (rather than cash-flow loans only), and fewer Homeland Security pat-downs and less government intrusions into our private lives?

At the very least, shouldn't we be looking for it?

If not, why not?

If we don't, how stupid are we? How green is it up where our heads are buried?

If we don't return home to America, our money woes will really be funny compared to where America will end up.

10 SEPARATION OF CHURCH AND STATE

Who participates in government *without* promotion of their cause?

To point at religion, whether it is some Baptist organization or the Salvation Army or an Order of Nuns representing the Catholic Church and claim they should have no seat at the table, is the epitome of not only wrong but dangerously wrong-thinking.

Especially, when unions, acorns and every other left-wing group, and the "regressive" air-heads who appear as "guests" in liberal-leaning church pulpits every Sunday, the liberal "news spews" on PBS, and fuzzy-wuzzy professors teaching socialist theories in classrooms on campuses all across America, are welcomed to the table with open arms (and generously funded from forced-open wallets of taxpayers) is stupid.

Let us all spell it together S-T-U-P-I-D! Not *thick, dense, ignorant, moronic, idiotic,* but plain ol' fashioned stupidity.

The worst American-based religions are die-hard unions, non-smokers, climate change greenies, movie porn stars, American Idol fans, atheists, yellow-dog dimocrats, liberal RINOs, Emily's List members, rap music devotees, bureaucrats, Hillary fans, and Obama supporters, *organized* effort to kill you or churches that urge their members to kill you, or doom you to Hell (if you're not a member), and the know-nothing TV anchor heads.

But all of these, and the others like them, are warmly welcomed to the table by the left.

Separation of Church and State, by the founding fathers, was to *prohibit* the state *sponsoring a specific church or religious order*, not religion in general. They were religious men who feared a "Church of England" – as they remembered an England under Catholic rule.

Today's progressives decry an individual belief in a forgiving Christian God, but forgive the extremes dominated by Muslim clergy and home-grown religious extremists; and become very eloquent about freedom of speech (and religion) if one utters a word of caution about Muslim extremism in America, or the building of a Mosque at Ground Zero.

Using "Church and State separation" against all Christian believers is a form of religion in itself. It is saying to one who holds a religious belief that "you cannot participate". It denies what a man may believe in or it is used to tell him how he must think, and it is a "kissing cousin" to the belief of radical Islam, which is more of a political belief than a religion.

One group seeks to deny participation to believers and the other seeks to deny participation to all non-believers.

Yet, the liberal/progressives/regressives *claim* they believe the door of government should be "open to all" and for all groups.

Except Christians.

It is a form of mental sickness.

The thing *they say* they fear the most is what they are *actually* promoting: What is the difference - in power and evil - between saying, "you cannot participate" or "you must participate"?

Both progressives and religious nuts are beyond belief (oops! that sounds almost religious...)!

Religion is about an individual's faith in a Supreme Being. Imposing, *by government force*, your belief in Mohammed or JFK or Obama or God is not religion. It is political evil.

Imposing, by government force, *your belief in government,* on another is a religion in itself, and it, too, is evil.

Demanding that government force others to live by your belief is evil.

The current espousing of "separation of Church and State" is a new code promoting nothing more and nothing less than the age-old argument for *more* government control.

Actually, behind all the talk about "separation of Church and State" is the debate for and/or against abortion.

But the debate over abortion is not about religion. It is a debate where both sides are arguing for *more* governmental control.

Somewhere along the way, the debate on whether government has the right to interfere *either way* got lost.

Isn't abortion a personal decision? What could be more personal? And where does one's religious belief gives one the right to interfere in another's personal life?

Why should government have any role to play, including the funding of any abortion activity, whether clinics or counseling?

It is a debate between those wanting government to stop abortions and those wanting government to approve abortions. Both sides are arguing for government control.

If government has the power to tell you that you cannot have an abortion, it has the power to tell you that you must have an abortion.

Do we really want a society where everything not forbidden is compulsory?

Be careful of what you want ... and be very careful about what you're really debating...

11 LIES OF INCOME INEQUALITY IN AMERICA

The 535 elected Democrats and Republicans (and the one Independent that votes with the Democrats) in Nutland, D. C., and sycophants in both parties, are lying about income inequality in America.

The inequality of the haves and the have-nots, the America that works and the America that does not, present a false argument over income, civic responsibility, greed and victimization.

It is not an argument over income inequality, but an argument between two parties who want to win elections.

One, the Democrats, engage in the politics of envy and class warfare. If you want it, the Democrats will take it for you. They are promoting the slavery of dependence and entitlement, of victim-hood and anger, the thinking that is the product of third world countries.

This philosophy was recently on proud display when President Obama pledged the rest of his term to fighting "income inequality."

Americans should be worried about *equal treatment.*

He noted that some people make more than others, and that some have higher incomes, and he said that is not just.

Republicans, in general, view income variations as the result of different choices that lead to different consequences. They claim those who choose wisely and responsibly have a greater likelihood of success, while those who choose foolishly and irresponsibly have a greater likelihood of failure. This is a message for responsibility and accountability; an argument that success and failure frequently manifest themselves in personal and family income inequality. Well, *duh...!*

But the Republicans only tell the story. They don't work to make it happen. They talk the game but, once in Nutland, D. C., join and hold hands with those who only are working to feather their nest.

And both parties blame the other one. They point to the recent years of growing disparity in the nation's average family incomes, and blame the other party for it.

These two philosophies divide America. And both contain lies of omission, as well as the more obvious ones.

They lie because the argument is more about staying in power and getting re-elected than it is about love of country – or about the need for equal treatment under the law, which leads to economic freedom and a free society.

Neither party today, neither argument, offers equal treatment under the law. Where economic choice leads to different economic outcomes. Both parties offer false arguments to cover their lies of omission about this lack of equal treatment under the law for the creation of economic opportunities or economic choice.

Both parties ignore it, and talk about the need for "fairness" and "income equality"; about creating good (time-card punching) jobs – which reassures Big Business that their favored status and subsidies and tax-breaks perks will continue.

But fairness and income equality are not in the Constitution, but *equal treatment under the law is . . .*

Of course, there will always be some measure of inequality in height, weight, family size, IQ, bone structure, inheritance, health, etc., or if

you are in a government-approved segment of society. For example, seldom do those in law enforcement pay speeding tickets, and seldom will private retirement accounts equal the benefits of government retirement accounts.

And there will always be those demagoguery experts who will try and maintain a perception of false inequality to manipulate the ignorant into voting for them.

As long as we depend upon government to make our choices, there will always be a false inequality.

But equal economic opportunity where free choices lead to different outcomes is not inequality.

Inequality comes when there is no equal opportunity for economic choice.

And there is no equal economic choice – no equal treatment under the law – none – when government determines who will succeed and who will fail.

When campaign contributions are the only choice.

There is no true option for success if there is no true option for failure. There is no equal opportunity to pursue happiness when government is holding you down while pulling up the other guy.

We built the greatest economic system the world has ever known, created the world's highest average family incomes. We did it by guaranteeing equal economic opportunity based on *equal treatment under the law.*

It was a system supported on a foundation of millions of small businesses: endeavors started, developed, and grown successfully by free men and women who had an equal opportunity for access to financing. Capital.

But today, our economy is in shambles, our small businesses are dying, jobs are being lost, and family income levels are dropping because both national parties have actively worked to eliminate equal economic opportunity.

They worked, lied and acted to eliminate financing for the nation's small businesses.

Government swapped equal economic opportunity for large cash-flow loans to Big Businesses; loans which taxpayers are forced to guarantee. Until that time, banks made loans based on assets, by which new businesses could be created (loans for land, building, equipment, inventory, and other assets were also a way to create personal and family savings). New businesses do not have a cash flow until after the doors open for business.

Only the greedy or brain-dead could fail to understand that
    (a) a new business does not have a cash-flow until after start-up, and
    (b) a national banking policy to deny access to capital for small business startups destroys the nation's economic foundation.

But this policy change was pushed by a few big banks, insurance companies and stock trading firms who could see their benefit from big fees generated by making Big Loans backed by a government guarantee. In exchange for approving the change in lending policy, both Democrats and Republicans benefitted, as large campaign contributions are always welcome.

The results are in...and both parties are accountable. We call it "crony capitalism". But it is more than that - it is State Capitalism, a partnership between Big Business and Big Government controlling economic opportunity and the means of economic production. It is American-styled socialism.

There is no Right to Equality Outcome, but there is a guarantee of "equal treatment under the law".

The inequality dividing us is not the differences in income, but in economic opportunity.

The words "fair play" are not in the Constitution, but free men in a free society have a right to equal economic opportunity – *under the law!*

You cannot have a free and open society without equal economic opportunity.

But our elected officials are ignoring Constitutional Mandates in order to feather their own nests by their by pandering to those who have money.

Those with tight grips on the power centers are lying to us. They are offering us what socialists have always offered their victims-to-be: More government, less freedom.

What both parties are offering are not solutions, but class warfare wrapped up in sound-bite lies of *fair play* and *inequality.*

There is no fair play or equality without equal treatment under the law.

12 THE WORLD-WIDE WEB

It ain't all peaches, cream and honey when you browse the World Wide Web.

Or when you use the latest in communications technology.

All in all, behind the easily accessed websites, and the latest smart phone, there's danger lurking out there. Some of the user-friendliest, most-easily accessed, enjoyable websites and more widely advertised, are actually the most dangerous.

As you sit in the comfort of your home or office and click your way through the offered listings and apps, you are immediately fair game that is sought by curiosity-seekers and all sizes and temperaments of parasites and predators.

Some that immediately take up your trail make the Predator – and Alien – behaviors seem more like that of a beloved household pet. After these real predators have devoured you lock, stock and barrel, they come after your wife and kids, other family members, all your friends, and their friends, and do the same to all of them.

After all those pickings, these parasites and predators are off on the trail from the scents they picked up during those meals.

They are always hungry.

When you take to the Internet or press your favorite app, there is more than just your safety at risk.

The instant of that first faint click sends the whiff of you to those waiting to violate your right to be let alone. The first thing these parasites and predators take is your privacy.

From that first click, wherever you go, where you visit, are the traps of cookies and GPS – and other technologies – that direct and control your experience on the sites you visit, force advertisements on you, and recognize you on your next visit.

Install the best virus and malware protection, set your privacy and security at the highest level, and you can't browse the Internet. Lower security and privacy standards and spend your time running disk cleanup, scans, and deleting all the potential electronic enemy-bugs you can or your computer bogs down.

Why is it all necessary? Because those who control the search engines demand it. Because the advertisers offering those "apps" demand it.

Modern communications drive home the fact that "there's no such thing as a free lunch."

Websites automatically receive from you your IP address, such internet-use information as the URLs of sites from which you arrive, the site you will visit when you leave the website, your type of browser, your operating system, your mobile provider, your mobile devices, your ISP (Internet Service Provider), and possibly, even information stored in your computer.

But the Internet folks, unlike those from over 250 different federal government agencies, can't follow you door to door or town to town and send your location to the interested parasites.

And the federal police boys and girls can also do these things, and more, to the providers of the internet and communications services.

There's no equal protection under the law.

But the parasites and predators you visit can retain the information you provide in connection with surveys, polls, third party services, or other third party research undertaken with or without your consent.

All of this is compiled and used in *their interest*, not yours!

The internet search engines are not your friends.

In fact, most search engines are the worst violators of privacy. They gather, keep and store information about you, your operating system, your likes and dislikes. And most times that a government agency or your local courts demand the information they have, they share it.

This holds true for your Internet Service Provider, too. Does your provider appreciate your business? Sure, but just not as much as they want to sell you something more, or their desire to cooperate with government.

You are on your own when picking a Service Provider and/or browsing the World Wide Web. You are asking to be spied on ... and there are hundreds of thousands spying on you every time you saddle up your mouse. There is not a right to privacy anymore.

You are being spied on.

IF you ain't demanding that your elected official protect your privacy rights, do you really care?

IF you claim you love freedom, or even if you really and truly do, you should beware of those promising you safe browsing and privacy protection. Especially, it they say, "We're from the government, and we are here to protect you."

They lie.

13 "THOU SHALT NOT..."

Thou shalt not... is a traditional ethical directive. Whether a professed believer or not, there is no doubt that our early American society created laws that followed the pattern of the ethics formulated within the Ten Commandants.

Today, those of the progressive/regressive faith tell us that these are "ancient ethics" – therefore, they are poorly suited as guidelines for governing our complex, crowded, and changeable modern world. Some even go so far as to complain that they are offended by the very sight of the Ten Commandments.

They tell us that to meet the challenges of this brave new world, we must have more statutory laws, which requires more administrative laws. (Statutory Law is a law passed by a legislative body; and administrative law consists of rules and procedures established or demanded by regulatory agencies.)

And too often, what we end up with was not the original intent of the law.

Naturally, with more laws, come more agencies.

With more agencies, come more bureaucrats seeking more power and more money, and seeing loopholes in the laws that free men and women use to try and escape their control. So, they create more controls, which mean more laws.

And the misguided tell us that this cyclic solution is the only solution.

How much of this argument is to secure more aggrandizement by (and for) those writing and interpreting and administering the laws is open to question. But it is a very small question – as courthouses are full of attorneys with differences of opinions.

There is not much question that we, as a nation, now have more laws than we need. And those creating the laws leave *waaaaay* too many details to the interpretation by bureaucrats.

The result is a confusing quagmire of statutory and administrative law. Both are feared for the obvious question that ancient Romans asked themselves: *Quis custodies ipsos custodes*? (Who shall watch the watchers themselves?)

And the administration of law is leading to a corrupt government overseeing a corrupt society.

John Adams, a founding father, said that America must be "...a government of laws and not men."

It should be obvious to all but those in mental straightjackets that those bureau administrators, and the bureaucrats beneath them, will act in corrupt ways, leading to a corrupted system...unless governed by strong, ethical leaders.

An example of such a fact is the IRS picking and choosing whom they will reward and whom they will punish.

Other examples include agencies that are invading the privacy and security of our private homes, our personal papers and our conversations; in the inability of Congressional committees to somehow find evidence of lying and misbehavior by government officers and offices (even as it is being done right before them); and by government's deliberate non-action to protect American lives.

'But Americans are repeatedly told, ad nauseam, that more laws are needed as our population increases.

This is not a justifiable concept – unless you accept the underlying premise that civilized behavior is worsening and that, as we grow more savage, the population needs to be controlled.

If this is a fact, then it is another example that government cannot do the job its' supporters claim it can do.

This argument that as human population increases, more laws are needed to control the population, or to tell the population how to act, has brought forth and continues to bring forth laws that tell us what we must do and how we must do it.

It is law that tells us what we must do; not law that restricts others from doing bad things to us.

We have abandoned the restrictive laws of "Thou shalt not..." for laws that enforce the demand "You will...."

We are limiting our possibilities and our hope for the future. The more likely scenario (read "fact") is that problems come from too much government, not increases in our population.

Laws that punished bad behavior for wrong-doing have given way to laws that reward doing wrong and that punish the pursuit of independent or non-conforming actions.

We have strayed from a philosophy of temperance in government to demanding that government do all things.

We are demanding our own destruction.

Today, we are living in a society where passing laws that demand conforming behavior, give exceptions to certain groups, establish different classes of people, place friend against friend, and play favorites are perpetual dangers.

We have passed the embryonic state in removing restrictions on the propagation of more government, and establishing infringements on personal liberty.

As each hungry and growing government tentacle slithers into law, each decade more and more citizens willingly accept more and more infringements on our liberty because they see it as controlling crime or keeping them safe or doing something else for them. They see no major loss to complain about.

The average voter has no idea how much government intrusions over the past three or four decades have eliminated equal economic opportunity, reduced personal choice, and infringed on their individual liberty.

They have nothing on which to base a comparison.

Therefore, each generation knows less and less of the difference.

Those who are (supposedly) the watchdogs of liberty, the media, don't realize it either; they are too busy making sure they look good on camera or having the quotes of their favorite politician polished for consumption by those they see as the great unwashed public.

For the American citizen, the main and foremost challenge now is to focus on corrective measures needed to keep the custodians of government honest.

We must find ways to prohibit easy ways to legislate and create more laws. Regardless of what we're told, not all gridlocks or stalemates are negatives. A dam that is holding back the floodwaters is a good and needful thing.

We need to stop talking about "issues" and start concentrating on principles.

Principles are important.

Issues are things that change quite often. Generally, any value they have is in the mind of someone who wants something from other people.

We need the principles of "Thou shalt not..." applied to the lawmakers, the administrators, our nation's judges, and the society we live in.

We must - again - teach the basics of our Constitution; why and how it came to be, and that it is a restriction on government and not a call for more government.

We, even non-believers, need to ask ourselves, where society would be – or where it is headed – without the *"Thou shalt not..."?*

14 MIGHT...

Might without responsibility or restraint is evil.

It is amazing that multitudes, who can believe that a law against those whom they see as a danger to others, such as smokers (or those who drink too much and drive) or even religious and racial discrimination, can believe that a Code of Conduct with penalties to restrain predatory business behavior is somehow wrong.

Consider, if you will, a situation where some young practical automotive mechanic develops a simple device that improves miles per gallon of gas by 40-percent when attached to a vehicle's fuel injection system.

The man has a product he conceived, researched, created and developed. It has the potential to make him rich and wealthy. He knows what's needed for manufacturing, production, and distribution.

He has the knowledge and the product. What he does not have is all the start-up money necessary for land, building, equipment, material inventory and operating capital.

He is not used to money in the large amounts he needs now, so he drops in to the bank where he has been a loyal customer for the last fifteen years. And the bankers tell him that banking rules do not allow them to loan on collateral - assets – and, as there is not an existing cash flow, they cannot lend him the money he needs.

But ...

... the bankers say, they can introduce him to some good people who probably would loan him the money in exchange for a small percentage for helping him to get the enterprise started. And they do.

This new bunch are a polite bunch, all smiles, full of friendly advice, and they know a firm of smart, world-class accountants who explain how to raise the money he needs by "going public". The smiling guys give him the needed cash to finance the initial stock offering for a small 30-percent equity. Now, we're are all in the same boat they say. And to show their confidence in him and his endeavor, they will take the time to serve on the board of his new company, if he would like, so that they will be in the picture if he ever needs their advice or help. And they'll do it just in exchange for a small, future stock option at a reasonable price.

It is up to you, they say, it is not a requirement.

Grateful for their interest and concern for his project, he agrees. And they prepare some paper documents and proceed.

At first, things go well. The young man works 18-hours a day and soon the money is coming in, almost as fast as it is going out. But the business is growing fast, maybe too fast. More and more production facilities are needed. After the second year, debt is high, and the guys counting the beans mumble about how the business is not, maybe, as financially stable as it should be.

So, the board, all good fellows with the business's interest at heart, think it really does need more money, which is okay as the product is the hottest thing to hit the auto industry since automatic transmissions and air-conditioning.

And since the money keeps rolling in - in increasing amounts every week – it's okay.

The young man is knocking down more in salary than he ever dreamed. Besides, it is the basic product that is important, not the money. So this is all fine, because it's clear to even those peddling stock in the business that the basic enterprise is going to be a money tree one day, and does it matter if another fifteen percent is signed over to his friends with the money? It is just shares of stocks.

Paper is not important.

But suddenly, those nice people are not so friendly. And then he finds out that paper in this new world is *everything*. Suddenly, it turns out that those bits of paper he signed with all those smiling people means he no longer owns *his business*. He doesn't own anything but a few shares of stock.

The idea, the intellectual property, the patent, the copyright, the locations, the manufacturing facilities, the warehouses - everything – including the bank accounts - now belong to them. But nothing illegal has taken place; it's just business.

And there is nothing he can do. There's no one to sue for legal protection, because everything is legal, somehow ... somehow. . .

...and in case you libertarians and progressives and conservatives are reading this, this is the way business is done under America's new State Capitalism, the bridge between Big Business and Big Government on the road to socialism.

But isn't it our government's Constitutional role to protect citizens from enemies without and within its borders? To protect against the unscrupulous behavior of those who have the *might* by which they prey on weaker members of society?

And isn't it our government's Constitutional role to also assure an equal opportunity (not the outcome, just the opportunity) for all citizens, not just a special few?

The so-called "financial institutions" of today only make large loans based on existing large cash flows in exchange for big fees and a part of the business (equity). A few short years ago, this was an outlawed, parasitic practice by Mafia types. It was one of the reasons that Congress, in 1970, passed the Racketeer Influenced and Corrupt Organizations (RICO) Act in an effort to combat Mafia groups.

Crimes under the Act include extortion, securities violations, mail and wire fraud, etc.

Then, less than 20-years later, in the late 1980s, Congress – through the Federal Reserve Board member banks – changed the lending laws to allow the "extortion" of equity from businesses needing money and that were likely to pay back the money it needed, plus interest.

Cash flow loans and demands for equity are policies that create opportunities only for a special class of people – those who already have money or access to it. It is the reason why those with money are increasing capital; and those without money are just increasing.

The result of State Capitalism is the lack of economic opportunity for most individuals to improve their lives by the acquisition of assets. When it comes to equal economic opportunities, there is no equal treatment under the law - which is, by itself, illegal.

Not all new small business startups require millions of dollars. But small asset-based loans are not available. Is there any wonder that capable and hard-working people are unhappy that high unemployment exists when small businesses, that have historically created the most jobs, cannot find startup capital?

Politicians in both parties now talk about "small businesses" having *net incomes* of $1.7 million annually. (It takes real talent to be that dumb; to fail to recognize this gap between perception and reality. Even today, after 30 or more years of raging inflation, most actual small businesses have net income below $100,000 annually.)

But voters who have swallowed the Big Lies of how honorable public service is, keep re-electing the same bozos to office, while listening to some expert making big bucks from State Capitalism tell us about the wonderful things that Big Government does for (to) us.

All which proves you can seldom underestimate the intelligence of the American voter.

15 WEED CONTROL

Obviously, any government is composed of men and women.

To a large extent, the actions of any government are a reflection of the beliefs of the men and women in the government.

The emphasis of government will be enhanced by the beliefs of those who direct and carry out the policies and functions of the unit of government they represent; the bureaucrats.

Any government governed by men and women without a belief in God, or some very solid core values, is a government of men lacking standards of behavior and moral inhibitions. It will be an amoral government; which should be feared.

One of the world's great (well, strongest) believers in centralized, collective government, Lenin, argued that some people are like weeds in a garden: They destroy the work of others, making the harvest or progress impossible. And like weeds in a garden, they need to be destroyed.

Liberals know the governmental programs they push would work, if it wasn't for all those weeds (who don't appreciate what those in government are trying to do for [to] them).

Like Lenin, today's misguided, confused "progressives" know that "weeds" need controlling, which is the reason for the rules and regulations contained in every government program.

This is the fallacy of liberal thought.

Rational beings advocate limited government.

Rational beings know that government's main purpose is weed control: (1) To protect us from foreign or locally-grown weeds, and (2) to do the very few things which we cannot do for ourselves.

And rational beings, recognizing that government is made up of mere men and women, worry that those in charge, who direct and carry out the mandates, may or may not have a belief or faith that requires of them responsibility for their actions and self-discipline on their behavior when it comes to weed control.

History demonstrates to rational and even semi-rational beings that centralized governments are big on weed control.

For instance, Lenin and his progressive cronies eliminated millions of what they viewed as Russian weeds; Hitler and his thugs did the same to the millions of humans that they saw as weeds in Germany; Castro's Cuba is big on weed control, bundling thousands in places where nothing can grow;

China (and those in charge today) have shown the world how to do weed control; and Bosnia, Somalia, Ethiopia, Yemen, Iran, etc., are big advocates of weed control ... and Somalia, Ethiopia and others starve their weeds. ISIS sees a world full of weeds.

History is replete with this fallacy of progressive thought.

Rational beings do not see themselves as weeds.

16 THE LIBERTARIAN QUESTION

Libertarians come across as straight shooters. Remarkably, especially for politicians, libertarians are constantly consistent in their ideas and public stand on issues.

Most of their arguments about lower government spending and taxation appeal to many voters. The ideas on less government and more individual freedom are sound, even to moderates and a lot of the left-leaning liberals. And any opposition to the unfettered financial powers of the Federal Reserve System sounds great to those of us worrying about budget deficits and policies that have lead to the destruction of economic opportunity for all Americans.

But for many of us, their opposition to military action against folks in other countries who do us wrong, sucks...

Their arguments generally show an empirical basis.

History demonstrates that many of those proposed solutions will work to the benefit of a free society, as most centralized governments never do. Thus, most of the ideas offer a solid foundation on which to build the kind of country free men would want to live in.

But there's the libertarian's damn pesky opposition to spanking an enemy determined to do us or our friends wrong. And their failure to acknowledge that economic opportunity is or should be available to all citizens (not just big business), is a problem.

Enemies exist, both outside and inside our borders.

Oh, we are in complete agreement that militarism for the sake of militarism is not what we should be doing. We agree that America has no right to be interfering in the way other countries want to run their countries, *but neither do they have a right to interfere in ours.*

But if they do more than talk, please . . .forget that "leave them alone" crap.

Agreed, America should never start military actions against another country; but if another country does or harbors those who commit a military or terrorist act against us, *they need reminding of the joys of the Stone Age.*

And **no** nation building, afterwards.

Yes, we understand there will always be that segment of American Good Souls who have given us North Korea, Vietnam, and now the mess in the Middle East, who believe we deserve to be murdered, beaten, raped, maimed, and otherwise attacked by the world's terrorists, thugs and two-bit dictators.

To retaliate, these good souls say, means that we, the USA, would be killing "the innocent" in those countries.

Regretfully, there will always be the weak-minded.

But are not most of those "innocents" responsible for their country's actions, their leadership, just as we are in our country?

If innocents settle for a leadership of terror, aren't they responsible for the terror? (Just as the "innocents" in America, who are pushing a system of socialism, are responsible for dragging everyone down into the maws of collective government.)

A worldwide understanding of an American policy (leave us alone and we'll leave you alone), and one or two examples of what happens if you don't leave us alone, is all that would be required to bring "peace and goodwill" to our little corner of the world.

There are bad people out there, and when they do something bad to us, they need to know what is gonna' happen to them when they do!

And we need American leadership with the political will to establish and enforce the policy *and the consequences!*

Then, there is the economy. Our politicians have allowed banks to become not just banks, but big financial institutions selling everything from insurance to stocks and bonds and – for a big fee – big cash-flow loans to big businesses.

Where is the opportunity for small business startups in such a rigged game?

So the question to Libertarians is, why should we vote for you if you see no reason to protect us from enemies outside and *inside* our borders?

17 THE PEOPLE'S BUSINESS...

America's prestige is at an all-time low.

And not just here.

During the last week of July, 2015, on the 29th and 30th, television showed former Senator and current Secretary of State John Kerry painfully hobbling around on crutches before Congressional committees and news reporters.

Then, on Saturday, August 1, 2015, Kerry was seen on television bouncing down a jet airliner's steps in Egypt, and during a series of meetings with Egyptian officials, seeking their support for the Iran sell-out in exchange for selling Egypt several F-16 Fighter Planes, there wasn't a crutch in sight.

Evidently, a miracle occurred when Kerry got away from Washington, D. C.

Wonderland, D. C. would be a better place without 'Lurch" K – but Egypt sent him back – they wouldn't have him.

Neither would any country with any sense.

But before Kerry, we had Honest Hillary Clinton waddling around the world, throwing her weight around as the Secretary of State, cackling about resetting "reset buttons", soliciting for the various Clinton money-raising Foundations, and otherwise destroying America's image as a sane nation.

For a number of months now, Democratic apologists are apologizing for Honest Hillary "doing something stupid" – wiping e-mails off her semi-private server and lying about how none of them involved national security. But it now seems that many of those e-mails came from five or more national security agencies, such as the CIA and the NSA.

Basically, the e-mails are top-secret, classified or not. The Department of State makes most of the designations, as it is almost impossible to classify one until after it's received. But the way Honest Hillary treated them was a danger to our national defense. But her supporters (mostly mentally deranged) claim she shows "strong leadership" qualities. They seem to forget so did Hitler and Stalin and Castro and Bin Laden, among others.

They also forget the results of that "strong leadership".

But foolish people say foolish things.

The Obama Administration refuses to investigate, and the Republican leadership, regardless of what they say, keep playing patty-cake with the supporters of more government – and refusing to strike sparks in the power structure by demanding an Independent

Prosecutor to seek answers to un-Constitutional Executive power and/or Honest Hillary's e-mails.

Doesn't the two-party system work great?

The nation's progressive-socialists should be happy.

After 50-or more years of basically getting what they wanted in foreign relations policies, however, the results are not in America's interest.

First, the liberal bunch successfully convinced most of us that if America became involved in a war – or a not-so-terrible police action – that our objective was not to win, but to resolve the conflict "peacefully".

And Americans lost their will to win.

But foolish people will do foolish things.

Based on Hope and Change, we elected the epitome of a progressive regressive for President, a politician who surrounded himself with like-minded idiots.

What? You object, you say? Well, look at his helpers and advisors, such as Rahm "Riot" Emanuel, the present 55th Mayor of Chicago; ol' Honest Hillary "Stand By Your Man" Clinton; John "Lurch" Kerry; Valerie Jarrett, senior adviser and rubber doll look alike; Lovely Lois Lerner, ex-IRS Commissioner and government-employee pinup; and a hosts of other administrative see-no-evil, hear-no-evil, say-no-evil socialists come to mind.

Unfortunately.

All we have are politicians who shirk from any danger to the position or office they hold, offering themselves as heroes protecting American interest. It is the action of cowards.

Those yearning for more government in control only want government in control of others.

None of those advocating for more government, advocate more control over themselves, only over the other guy.

It's always the other guy who needs controlling.

Never do they ask, "Who will control the controllers?"

But controlling people is not the government's business. Its job is to do the things that people need – not want – *need* it to do. The Constitution is to assure that our government is to work for us – not us for it.

The people's business is making sure the government is working for us.

Fifty states, not 57, comprise the United States of America.

There are about 18,500 elected officials governing these 50 states; and there are just over 100,000 governmental units in these 50 states.

All together, voters elect around 500,000 individual parasites to the county, municipal, village, township, and special district governments to go along with the President, Vice-President, 100 Senators, and 435

Representatives. Parasites because they live off the tax dollars they suck from our wallets.

The Washington, D. C. bunch alone are now costing us over $1.4 trillion every year – not counting the mounting debt they continue to pile up.

But these 500,000-or so elected individuals are our responsibility. We know we elected them. Those that they appoint and employ are *their* sole responsibility, but guess whose pockets that pay comes from!

Have we no common sense?

The people's business is politics.

Do we know how to take care of our political business?

And the bottom line is that government seldom solves any problem; it makes it worse.

If this causes you to roll your marbles until the red shows and grind your pearly whites, and fizz, name three problems government has solved?

Thanks to those we elected and our apathy for holding them accountable, all we have for a national economic base are a few large conglomerates and monopolies producing enormous amounts of money, which they share generously with both major political parties, the U. S. Congress, highly-placed law enforcement officials, and financial buddies.

Economic opportunity has been reduced to joint ventures, which means giving equity to a financial or governmental insider.

It doesn't matter if you're starting a new company or buying an established firm, you are going to give someone a substantial share for peanuts.

It is a national disgrace.

It is a also a national disgrace that only financial and governmental insiders have access to economic opportunity.

Oh, sure, there are a few hustlers, con-men, and BS-artists armed with MBAs, a recommendations from low-friends in high places, and lots of high energy nervousness and unfounded egos, playing Monopoly with other people's money. And a growing number of economic qualifiers carrying large satchels of drug money made possible by "a war on drugs."

A war as successful as the "War on Poverty."

As The Donald proclaimed: We are not good at winning anymore. (Proving that anyone can be right sometime.)

We fought to a pitiful "political" draw with an under-armed and economically dead North Korea; which still has a starving population of robots regimented into slavery by an obvious nut with atomic and nuclear weapons.

Later, headed by LBJ and Bob McNamara, our political leaders over-rode military knowhow and military capability – and military willingness to win - for our first complete military loss in Vietnam.

And now, what are we doing "nation building" in the middle east?

Nation building?

Thanks to our political leadership, as a country we lost our political will in Korea, our pride and confidence in Vietnam, and now, we've lost our minds: We are "nation building" in countries that hate us.

Nation building in countries that hate us? Where large segments of the population hate not only us, but also each other? We are wasting billions and billions in nations that are dedicated to not only killing us, but each other?

How utterly s-t-u-p-i-d can we be?

What happened to the American standard of "walk softly, but carry a big stick"?

What is wrong with a philosophy of "don't start it, but do some serious damage if someone else does." We need a principle of "We won't bother you, if you won't bother us. But if you do, we're gonna' kick your butt back to the Stone Age."

And mean it.

But today, you can kill – murder – and maim thousands of us and we will "build your nation"?

If we haven't reached the end of stupidity, but we can see it from here –

Bombs we got. Munitions we got. Knowhow we got. But guts and a political will are in very short supply – we're overflowing with mental, physical and emotional cowards.

But no one cares.

As a nation, we are in our 4th and 5th go-around of breeding and raising emptiness and shallowness to match that of Nero and Caligula. The only difference is they fiddled while we have those damn 'git-tars'.

We have generations of vapid and self-centered spoiled brat geniuses stuffing their bodies with surplus calories and starving their minds and emotions and worshiping at the feet of some superstar with the same or less talent than those doing the worshiping; a case of stupidity recognizing stupidity and feeling comfortable with it. And a society proud of it.

We have government leaders who believe in and are strongly committed to "diplomatic conversation" on international matters, but are completely committed to "Peace through superior firepower" domestically.

We're idiots.

We spend hours in airports being patted down and felt up for a fingernail clipper while Patriot Act and Homeland Security "safety experts" check the diapers of ninety-plus year old great-grandmothers for bombs and refuse to profile those who are boarding who are matches or near matches for terrorists. And while these "safety experts" are treating us so unthinkingly rude (government jobs require government ways), their bosses in Nutland, D. C., are working desperately to keep our borders open and find ways of making illegals legal.

We treat American citizens as outlaws and those in other countries (who are trying to destroy us) as "reasonable, well-intentioned, peaceful people".

We're complete idiots.

There are actually a large number of people placing their lives on *Facebook*, and who spend hours *"tweeting"*, who find it difficult or impossible to believe there are millions and millions of people who do not care what they happen to be doing or whether they're enjoying it. They are either so self-centered or bone-deep stupid that this possibility never occurs to them.

And they vote.

Worse. They think they have an opinion.

And we're all so far gone that few of us realize that we're being swept into economic slavery under a system of State Capitalism, a socialistic partnership between Big Business and Big Government. (And headed for fewer Big Businesses and an even Bigger Government.)

But why worry?

We can stand together mindlessly screaming

"U-S-A! U-S-A! U-S-A!"

until our country has lost all of its national identity.

American has lost Her way. So it's time to start seriously asking what is the difference among the big bad three: Socialism and Communism and Fascism.

You get either of the three with just plain political stupidity.

Everything else is just political window dressing.

Shouldn't we know the difference among the three?

We ask because years ago, while arguing with a college professor discussing the role of government economic development activities, we argued that the new government-sponsored-and-funded Community Action Programs were designed by Washington's socialists planners to replace the nations more conservative-leaning local chambers of commerce. This was part of our argument for limiting government's role in local economic development activities.

And the liberal, progressive SOB called me "a right-wing fascist".

Imagine!

But even while still green around the ears, and wondering what the stars could see, the world offered enough other bright colors to see that, regardless of the professor's words, fascism was just another system of government control.

That professor – as others have – claimed that socialism is to the left and that fascism is to the right.

Socialists, who want to be viewed as being in the middle, are selling soft soap and can't stand a bad press. So they threw fascism, with its Nazi connection, under the socialist bus. This way, they can claim that "nationalism" (a strong support of one's country, like patriotism) is fascist, and that it is "right wing" stuff.

Such claims are designed to undercut support for those *extremists* who believe in limited government; those whom the progressives accuse of being "against the people."

Therefore, they push the perception that socialism is the "middle" between communism and fascism.

Such reasoning makes no sense.

First, each and all of the Big Three systems demand individuals support the state and give control of the means of production to the state.

But arguments for limited government are arguments against the state.

Franco's Spain and Mussolini's Italy were Fascist states. As such, they certainly were not proponents of individual liberty or the rights to private property ownership or the freedom of economic choice.

How could any thinking person arrive at a conclusion that a belief in government control is the same as a belief in limited government?

Dictionaries focusing on socialism declare it is, in general, a political and economic theory where the state owns or regulates the means of production, distribution, and exchange. Socialism, its supporters say, can coexist with private and personal property. But so does fascism, the fascists claim. And socialism and fascism coexist with private property as controllers and masters, basically, like communism.

If you control it, does it matter who owns it?

If you own it, but I reap the benefit, who benefits?

Franco and Mussolini were squeezing the same sour lemon as Stalin, Hitler, Chairman Mao, Peron, the Castros, Hassan Rouhani, Kim Jong-un, and so many other "compassionate" leaders that, all together, they would fill Hell up to the brim.

And they should.

Even no-brainers should be able to figure out who will be those controlled in any centralized system of government.

The difficulty is figuring who will be in control and the master of all that no-Hope and no-Change?

Communism, which acts on the same theory as socialism and fascism, gets the bad press. Communism, as Marx wrote in The Communist Manifesto in 1848, "can be summed up in the single sentence: Abolition of private property."

There is no pretence about ownership or ownership rights.

As a political theory it calls for a class war leading to a society in which all property is owned by the state, and each person works and is paid based on his/her abilities and needs. (There's no pretence, like America bailing out those "too big to fail"?)

Peel away all the adjectives promoting socialism and fascism down to results, and all you have is communism without all the lipstick and make-up. There's no practical difference. Socialism and fascism are soft-peddled communism because the promoters do not want to be associated with the overt use of force.

But neither are socialism or fascism safe alternatives to communism: The murders of some 100-million prove that. In any central system of raw power, the brutes will always claw their way to the top.

A crusty citizen of San Angelo, in far West Texas, relates the way the difference in Joseph Stalin's Russian Communist Party (Socialist) and Adolph Hitler's NAZI Party (National Socialist Party) were explained to him when he was in Junior High School. One of his teachers told him that the basic difference was that the Communists believed that the State owned everything and, thereby, controlled everything; WHEREAS, the Nazi Party (German National Socialist) believed in the private ownership of property BUT the owners had to run for their lives or live according to what the State mandated. So in the long run, he said, I can't see a hell of a lot of difference in living under either system.

"You still MUST obey the National Government or suffer the consequences," he said.

Thanks to his teacher, he has it right.

All collective systems operate with the belief that the state is supreme and all activity should be for the benefit of the state. The "common good" – so often spewed – is to justify some controlling activity that confines and forces people to their usefulness to the government's purpose. It is control for the benefit of the state without regard for the individual.

Theory and propositions for government become juxtaposed in an unrealistic search for some unknown utopia, where everybody is equal (in every way); where assets and income are divided equally (if necessary, every other Friday); where there are no unfulfilled needs (our kids are not ugly); and everybody lives happily ever after (while eating their fill of American Apple Pie).

But these promises will always fail, because government cannot fulfill all the yearnings of individuals. There will always be yearnings. And this failure of government to operate as promised – as government can never do what it promises – creates artificial divergences (in name, but not form). A new name signifies *this change* to the system will work.

(Throw in some big words that can mean what you want them to mean here and you, too, can have a new name for an old system of terrible government, one where might makes right.)

This is why all the various names for collective and controlling government systems exist. Each nomenclature is some small divergent that makes each system different (or so the collectivists claim) as the core stays the same.

And, hope you caught the word "collectivists"? The control of resources and people requires assets and labor to support the army of bureaucrats collecting the taxes or running the money printing press and, in general, enforcing the rules. Regardless of name (socialism,

fascism, or communism), each is a collective system. Therefore, the supporters are collectivists.

Of course, some socialists or misguided economists argue that socialism can work, by claiming that Hitler and the Nazi party brought Germany out of a much longer and greater depression than the rest of the world (because of WWI), and surpassed the growth of the other industrialized nations of that time. And they tell us that Il Duce" made the trains in Italy run on time."

No one but socialists, fascists and communists can do it?

Daniel Balderdash!

They conveniently forget that it did not work out too well for Germany or Mussolini's Italy. Did it?

If the results of what happened to Germany and Italy under those two is your idea of success, bless you, and may the staff at the home treat you well. Maybe you'll regain your mind soon. . .

If not, you can always be elected to Congress.

Most of modern Europe is socialist - and America is moving their way. Fast.

The Democratic Party is one mass of echoing socialists proudly calling themselves progressives. "Washington Republicans" are cowards and appeasers who are scared silly of Democrat demagogues, but will quickly attack an advocate for limited government.

And the so-called Tea Party has no idea how to form a coherent message to stop America's lemming rush to the left.

We are a nation of government supporters spouting loudly about "the public benefit" and the "common good" and shouting "USA, USA, USA!" at some circus, while Congress pours tax dollars into a war on poverty that was doomed to failure before it started.

Today, our nation's courts ignore Individualism, the foundation of our American exceptionalism, and the priority of human dignity and rights, as set out in our system embodied in the U. S. Constitution.

Everything we are doing is for the *commune*.

For what we are told is *the common good*.

We're a nation Spying, Lying and Dying.

History, ancient and modern, proves America's endorsement of and our rush to join the Big Bad Three.

Keeping us a free nation is the people's business.

Sadly, we're not attending to business.

19 SAY "NO"!

Cliches, posters and slogans espousing freedom, less government, and "We're Mad As Hell And We're Not Taking It Anymore," are not the answers to stopping an ever expanding centralized, federal government.

Neither are marches expressing outrage over the growth of government, which are countered with marches by those who want an expanding federal government.

Only the importer of shoes wins -

The only answer to less government is having an electorate smart enough to say "No!" to more government.

For skeptics who think that government is the answer to most problems, the Bill of Rights was established because most of the Founding Fathers feared the Constitution did not go *far enough* in restricting or limiting the central government. As usual, they were right.

As there has been throughout history, there are those today who believe they are, as Byron so sarcastically wrote, ""The twice two thousand for whom the world is made..."

Socialism is a political philosophy of "special favors for special people." What foolish believers in government forget is that they will not always be one of the "special people."

But as the man said, "You can't fix stupid."

To stop government expansion of regulatory slavery, forget the noble-sounding promises of government; forget the nonsense that "government always does good things." We know different. If we look at the world around us, and if we think, we know that government is more often evil than good.

The top priority of government is to protect itself. The larger government becomes, the greater is its desire to expand even more - and the more it will do to protect itself.

More and more, we have those in government and those who want more Government believing that voters will not always vote "in their best interest" – and that more would be accomplished if those who did not understand what was in their best interest would get out of the way.

This line of foolish thinking by believers in government would, for instance, produce voters who would have great physical health, be capable of hard work, but with their thinking stunted or shaped and directed in a particular direction.

This, as repugnant as it is in concept, is almost within today's capabilities.

It's no secret that science is already cloning animals, that "test tube" babies are an accepted fact, and gene and DNA manipulations are daily experiments in many medical laboratories.

The obvious potential for developing a human being designed for a limited range of work or thought beyond that of "now" and "this way" is within today's real possibilities.

Artificial breeding techniques are no longer new, they are a part of current society. We can change or alter the breed of animals, insects, fish, fowl, and even the food we eat, and do it every day. Scientists are experimenting with developing entire life cycles - from insect to animal - carried out by artificial means in an artificial environment.

These are experiments with dangerous eventualities; and currently we lack abilities to prevent the power of science from expanding on the interference with nature.

History proves that there are always those with only the vision to obey the government and demand that others do so voluntarily (or they will throw you in jail or kill you). There is little in their philosophy to prevent creation of human robots to serve a world state.

There have always been, and are now, those who want an expanding and much more powerful government.

What the foolish forget, or hope that the majority of us forget, is that the States created a governmental system for the United States of America. The states created the central government.

Everything they fought for was to restrict the power of an all-powerful centralized government.

Omnipotency, unlimited power, was the last thing the Founding Fathers intended. They had just fought the Revolutionary War to escape such power from Britain and their main concern was to prevent a recurrence here in America.

The framers of our Constitution knew, and feared, a powerful centralized government. They were living the results. And in their fear of centralized government systems, they refused to give a federal government the power to expand or assume power wherever and whenever it felt like it.

As detailed in Article 1, Section 8, of the Constitution, the federal government was to be discrete and have very limited, enumerated powers.

A majority of the states demanded a supreme law to establish basic and fundamental rights for all future generations: Rights that would never be violated by government. During the months of debate, key states, and powerful delegates such as Patrick Henry, would not support the formation of a new government if the Constitution did not contain such a Bill of Rights.

So the Framers of our Constitution came up with ten God-given freedoms that were, and would forever be, held inviolable by our government.

The states created the federal government. By understanding that the States were the creator, it should be easy to acknowledge why anything not included in the Tenth Amendment is "reserved to the States respectively, or to the people."

It was to protect the power, sovereignty, and the autonomy of the States. This amendment underscores the entire purpose of the Constitution – to limit government, as it forbids the federal government from becoming more powerful than the "creator" (the states).

Anything not mentioned in Article 1, Section 8, in the Tenth Amendment, is *"reserved to the States respectively, or to the people."*

The states formed the federal government, not the other way around.

How can anyone rationally believe that the States intended to form a new government to control and command the States at will?

Nothing could be farther from the reality.

But the foolish believers in government claim that the Constitution is outdated. They claim it is a document needing constant change to meet a changing world. But these are foolish claims by foolish individuals.

Once we lose the structural protection of our constitutional system of checks and balances, which protect citizens from both the federal and the state governments, we will be a lost society.

The Constitution, the supreme law of the land, guarantees the rights of people.

Those who clamor for changing the Constitution are arguing to remove the structural protection for individual rights. The last thing citizens should be doing is removing the checks and balances that keep both state and federal government at bay.

Once we weaken the structural protection of the Constitution, we will lose our structural protection of liberty. We will be subject to federal control.

Today, all three branches are in violation of our Constitution:

- The Administrative departments are issuing directives and mandates requiring the States and their local communities to address particular problems; and it commands the State officials, and those of their political subdivisions, to administer or enforce federal regulatory programs that affect the life of every citizen.

- The Judicial branch is *creating law*, based on personal agendas of the individual justices, outside their Constitutional mandate. Some justices are pushing consideration of *Shari'a* and other law foreign to mandates in the U. S. Constitution.

- Congress has sold their authority and responsibility for a "go along to get along" policy of electability over principle, and betraying the trust of the American people. Along with the Administrative and Judicial branches, this Legislative branch is creating too many poorly conceived regulatory laws that infringe on Constitutional restrictions.

While such violations are fundamentally incompatible with our constitutional system of dual sovereignty, we tolerate their issuances and accumulation. We refuse to look or consider where we may be going. *Or why.*

Perhaps, it is already too late for such considerations: Our thoughts already shaped, stunted, specialized, and directed to accept a changing Constitution, the results of a government grant to some progressive scientist doing artificial test tube experiments in some far off university's laboratory.

Or more likely, years of progressive classroom instructions on how to achieve dream world benefits under a centralized government.

Like scientists manipulating nature, socialists are experimenting with the nature of our government.

America's socialists are pushing dangerous eventualities; and currently we lack the wisdom or the mental fortitude to prevent those we have elected, and those they have appointed to positions of power, from expanding their interference with our Constitutional rights.

Government can do anything it wants to until someone says, "NO"'.

Our Constitution – until or unless *we* change it – allows *us – encourages us –* to say "NO" to government.

It is time to say it.

20 CONGRESSIONAL RETIREMENT PACKAGES

In 1980, the salary for a Congress "person" was $60,662.50 – compared to the $174,000 they now are knocking down.

Since they control the nation's purse strings, could this almost 300-percent increase be because of inflation?

For some years, they have given themselves built-in pay increases for doing a lousy job of overseeing the economy? Or, maybe, so that they don't have to vote to give themselves an annual pay raise?

But it's not just the salary – and to some extent, the Congressional retirement and health care benefits – for the part-time job it is supposed to be: it's the job they're not doing.

There is a lot of talk about salaries, perks, and other things, and they are, indeed, generous by the standards of most workers. Especially, when compared with health plans offered by private employers.

The Federal Employees Retirement System (FERS) offers more choices — in fact, "the widest selection of health plans in the country," according to the Office of Personnel Management.

But for the most part, benefits for Congress are similar to those of any federal employee, although there are differences.

We do not claim that the information and data contained herein is a full and complete survey of all Congressional pay, retirement plans, health benefits and perks. It's only offered as an attempt to gain a more accurate picture of some benefits enjoyed by members of Congress at the taxpayer's expense. Any mistakes that may be included may be our fault, or the lack of transparency in sections of the FERS information supposedly containing how the retirement plans work.

First, keep in mind that nearly all Congress members are covered by (FERS), which has three parts (and members do have a few extra "perks"):

(1) Social Security. Members of Congress have Social Security taxes withheld from their pay like other workers, and are eligible for retirement benefits beginning at age 62.

The benefit formula is based on "high-3 average pay." This is calculated by averaging the highest basic pay over any 3 consecutive years of service; and generally, is calculated according to the usual formula.

(2) The Thrift Savings Plan: A 3% Savings Plan contribution is matched with another 4% from the employer (the government's taxpayers).

This is a "defined contribution" plan, similar to the 401(k) plans common in the private sector. But there is a difference: Whether *or not* a Congressperson chooses to save anything, the government contributes 1 percent of their base pay to the savings plan.

(3) Special Retirement Supplement: Members of Congress, along with other people on the federal payroll, receive a traditional "defined benefit" pension, something that is available to only a small percentage of private-sector workers.

A Member of Congress or Congressional employee, with at least 5-years of Congressional service, receives this annual unreduced annuity at age 50 with 20-years of service or at any age with 25-years of service.

If you are a Member of Congress or a Congressional employee, with at least 5-years of service, the annuity will be:

1.7% of highest-3 average pay, times years of Congressional service up to 20-years, plus 1.0% of the highest three average pay times for any other service.

According to the Congressional Research Service, *in October 2006* this annual average pension for a retired member of Congress who served under FERS was $35,952 (compared with the current $174,000 salary for active members).

An estimated retirement benefit of all three (or more) retirement perks under FERS is not attempted here, as transparency is lacking on the total percentages applied under each of the benefit plans, as the benefits depend upon each current and former member's respective age and term of service.

For instance, members of Congress can begin drawing their full pension at age 62 if they have completed five years of service, at age 50 with 20 years' service, or at any age with 25 years' service. Or they can collect a reduced pension with 10 years of service at ages 55 to 57, depending on their birth year.

OTHER PERKS: Members of Congress participate in the Federal Employees Health Benefits Program along with about 8 million federal workers, retirees and their dependents.

They are also eligible for Medicare, and pay the same 1.45 percent tax on their salary as do other federal workers, but there are some medical benefits beyond those available to regular federal workers.

For an annual payment of $503, members can receive routine care from the Office of the Attending Physician, which has facilities in the Capitol. Recent reported services include physicals and other examinations, on-site X-rays and lab work, physical therapy and referrals to medical specialists.

In addition, current members (but not their dependents) can receive medical and emergency dental care at military hospitals and clinics. In-patient care is covered by FERS insurance, but outpatient care *is free* if it's performed at facilities in the national capital region, such as Bethesda Naval Hospital in Maryland or Walter Reed Army Medical Center in the District of Columbia.

Miscellaneous: Before 1984, Congress was covered by the old Civil Service Retirement System and members were not required to pay into Social Security — nor could they get a Social Security benefit.

But at present, all members of Congress must pay into Social Security, including nearly 50 currently serving members *who were first elected before 1984.*

Members of Congress are not affected by proposals for pay freezes for federal employees — Congress sets its own pay scales separately, and in 2009 and 2010 voted to forgo its usually automatic annual pay increases.

But not since ... as it is hard to make financial ends meet when you're only making about 3.5 times the wages of the average voter.

A member who leaves office before serving five years because of an election defeat or resignation is not eligible for a pension. And any member convicted of a crime such as bribery, fraud, racketeering or perjury for acts committed after September, 2007, is ineligible.

All in all, not a bad deal. Especially, when reimbursed expenses are added in ... and free haircuts and those "fact finding trips" that seem to be more about vacations than congressional business.

Actually, in truth, only a few tight-lipped actuarial type bureaucrats know what these other "perks" cost us poor taxpayers . . .

As seen by government, the first job of government is to take care of government.

The job of a Congressman is to perpetuate the system.

Voters have a lot to answers for –

Our nation's $19-plus trillion national debt demands term limits.

The destruction of Constitutional mandates demand term limits.

Voters have allowed those in "public service" to create themselves (and a few special people) as America's royal family.

Equal treatment under the law has been ignored for too long by those we elect to office and those they appoint to departments, agencies, and the nation's courts.

Term limits exist at the ballot box.

You might want to remember that . . .

21 BIG OIL, ETC.

Here is a lop-sided glimpse of America's – and the world's – most secret business.

So, in no particular order (only with sub-titles), we begin:

Robins and Energy:

Every year, when Spring has sprung forth and the red, red Robins are bob, bobbin' along, gas-powered vehicle owners are warned that we are living at the edge of a dark age.

We break out in a sweat, ride around in our SUVs with the air conditioning on and weep, and send our money to the climate change bunch.

Our days and nights become haunted by visions of month after month of walking down vacant miles of super highway concrete without a gas-motorized vehicle or an adult beverage in sight.

Sometimes in these dreams of a bright tomorrow, where any change in climate is controlled by (we're told) a benevolent government, in the far distance we see a wild drifter on an algae-powered motor scooter disappearing into a dust storm and, at other times, we are passed by a few hardy types in wobbly-tired wagons pulled by a team of Billy Goats. And a horde of starved creatures stare at us imploringly as we, nibbling on a wild carrot, pass them by.

Every year, the Good Life enjoyed from the production of fossil fuels is transformed by government agency and oil company news releases and publicity handouts to a Life on the Edge of a No-Tomorrow.

Every year, the same Robin Hoods sing the same song at the same time of the year, but tomorrow never comes.

Surely, it isn't because it is just in time for the travel season?

But *Oh*, aren't we dumb enough to buy it?

The energy companies know this.

We've proven it to them time after time.

Since the mid-1970s, we've swallowed every oil shortage, all the international conflicts, unknown tomorrows, hangnails, stumped toes, minor and major drug-induced nightmares, and the worlds of uncertainties the oil companies and the politicians and the dog-leg schemers of State Capitalism have thrown at us.

It's like every lame, lying excuse has never been heard before and we reach to open our wallets.

You would think, after all this time, that all this is not news!

It is so obvious that there is not a shortage of oil and gas that even the oil companies and politicians have quit trying to sell that nonsense.

Why, a somewhat reasonable individual might wonder, can't the politicians and the energy companies get together? If you know there is a big bump in the road you consistently travel, why would you insist on repeatedly hitting it?

You wouldn't. But the energy providers claim they are surprised by the same old bumps in the same old road every year. Why?

Do you think profits have anything to do with it?

Is old Supply and Demand at work?

Or greed?

The energy companies have a monopoly on being the energy providers. Those you elected to public office gave these providers this monopoly or conglomerate power. It doesn't matter what it is, what segment of the energy economy – oil, gas, electricity, solar, or our new love (but extremely costly) "green" – it is now a monopoly.

The politicians sold out for a campaign contribution or a high-paying job for a family member or loved one(s).

You either play ball with us, Energy Providers tell the politicians, or you don't play.

What, you ask without hope, as the sweat pours down your face, can I do about it?

Well, first, if you insist on sending the same ol' boys and girls off to Nutland, D.C., there's nothing you should try and do.

If you have never expressed your disgust about the prices you're forced to pay at the pump or never let your elected folks know that the policies they allow the Federal Reserve Board to force on us simple folks are inflationary, there's nothing you should even try and do ... you've done enough.

Next, it is the responsibility of your local city council members to approve or disapprove every request by energy and TV cable firms for an increase in rates.

Your local electricity, gas, telephone and cable TV companies are Franchises, operating in your city with your city's approval. And if you're happy that your local city councilperson gives these local providers their blessing, there's not much you can do when these companies raise your rates (but you can feel good about yourself for supporting your community).

And last, if you've done nothing, when the energy providers come to sheer your wallet, just hunch your back, pull your neck in, and say, *baa-a-a-a*.

Big Oil: *(Times are getting Hard, boys, money's getting scarce!)*
[NOTE: The following was published on a website we had a few years back. The information was developed first for an article back in the early 1990's; revised in 2001, again in 2005 and, again, in 2009. It is included here, because the same damn things still apply. We never learn...]

Each year, Big Oil - as exemplified by Exxon-Mobil - sets a new record for income.

In '05, when higher gas prices put many consumers in an economic crunch, Exxon's net profit rose 43-percent to a fresh mark of $36.1 billion, on income of $371 billion. Profits increased to another new record in 2006, again in '07 and '08, and are up about 12% for the first six months of 2009.

In this time frame, consumers have been paying a very high price for gas at the pump. And for the increased costs of transporting the products we need from one area to another – Of course, consumers pay for everything.

Big Oil enjoys our pain at the pump, pumping up the price, letting it drop, taking speculator's profit both ways...

In 2007, when releasing the information that they had made more money, in any year, than any other corporation, ever, Exxon took out ads in five major newspapers to claim the year's profit "is relatively moderate."

The American Petroleum Institute, an industry political and lobbying group, bought ads in seven national newspapers to make the claim that oil and gas industry profits "are moderate."

What they were telling the consumer was, in essence, kiss where I can't: This is our story and we're sticking to it.

The oil industry prefers to muddy the waters by concentrating on other industries' profit margins.

They also like to spotlight their costs. But what they really like, and what they are really good at doing is taking care of those in high places with accounting tax write-offs. For instance, part of Exxon's 2005 costs included outgoing Chief Lee Raymond's $82-million plus for the year and another $100 million plus retirement package.

And, yes, such costs as this make it difficult for the oil companies to make more than "a moderate" profit.

A Center for Public Integrity reported in 2003, that the international oil and gas industry had lavished more than $440 million over the previous six years on politicians, political parties and lobbyists in order to protect its interests in Washington.

Other key findings included that between 1998 and 2003, the industry spent more than $381 million on lobbying activities, and another $67 million in campaign contributions in federal elections.

The industry exerts its influence in other, less obvious ways, including membership on the National Petroleum Council, a commission formed to advise the energy secretary.

U.S.-based oil and gas companies have nearly 900 subsidiaries located in tax haven countries, such as the Cayman Islands and Bermuda.

And guess the leader in spending for lobbyists to plead its case with official Washington, D.C., over the past six years? Yes. You guessed it: The world's largest oil company, ExxonMobil, spending $55 million, was the leader in lobbying costs.

No wonder it is hard to make more than "a relatively moderate profit."

Other big spenders on Washington, D.C., occupiers included ChevronTexaco ($32 million), Marathon Oil ($29 million), British oil giant BP ($28 million), and British-Dutch behemoth Royal Dutch/Shell Group ($27 million).

Other noteworthy entries on the list include the top industry group, the American Petroleum Institute, which portrays itself as a non-profit independent, ($20 million), and Occidental Petroleum ($12 million).

No wonder lawmakers are reluctant to dig too deep into how markets can be and are manipulated, and the extent insider trading plays in the price of oil and gas futures. Any retrospection on the so-called "market price volatility" doesn't lend itself to any worthwhile investigation – if you want to keep benefiting from campaign and lobbyist spending.

"Ah, there's the rub," as Willie S. said. Lawmakers speechify grandly and tediously; sound and fury, signifying nothing.

The ones getting the lion's share of the money divert the questions to our being dependent upon foreign oil. And they are the ones who are eager to throw in the need for tax credits and write-offs to stimulate domestic development and production.

The ones who feel they aren't getting their fair share of the money, demand that profits be returned to the government to underwrite a favorite social program or two. (Which, when you think of it, is really a nice touch of blackmail: Do you want to pay a little to me – or a lot more in taxes?)

It is all rhetoric.

The fast-money boys, those who hold the license to collect part of the investment going in and coming out, live off the wide swings in market prices. They are some of the companies' greatest apologists.

"Geopolitical tensions remain," said a leading energy analyst at Purvin & Gertz in Singapore. "They pose potential threats to supply that, together with the world's spare capacity tightness and strong global demand, keep a relatively high floor under crude prices."

Gentlemen, when have "Geopolitical tensions" not existed?

Victor Shum, the energy analyst, made his remarks at a January, 2006, meeting of OPEC. "I have no control over prices," he said. "We accept that they are high, and of course, we want them to come down."

Of course, you do! But forgive our skepticism.

Almost without fail, stock market experts and advisors urge small investors to "buy oil."

"Oil is the new dollar," these experts claim. Well, forgive us, again. But the more often oil prices swing, and the wider they swing, and the higher the price of the stock, the more money from fees and commissions finds its way into the pockets of brokers.

Every seller and buyer of energy futures repeat the same manta: "I have no control over prices." This is the same weary battle cry of every crook charged with shady doings in the financial world.

It is the same lame-brain excuse peddled by the oil industry and their spokes people: "We have no control over prices. . ."

Well, isn't it time we found out just who does?

For a hundred years, even during the war years, gas and oil were a stable resource. But uncertainty – speculation – on oil and gas futures as a commodity entered the marketplace in the early 1990's.

The price run-ups and run-downs during the industries' "artificial shortages" of the 1970s and 1980s opened the door to present day price manipulations.

When "shortages" couldn't be sold to the general public, the nation's politicians and fast-money boys become convinced, with donations from the oil and gas industry easing the way, that oil and gas – with development and production and transportation and refining and delivery and wholesale outlets and retail outlets all controlled by a few monopolies – should be opened to speculation.

When you have billions of dollars to play with, and total control of the commodity, how smart do you have to be to manipulate the market?

With that kind of money available, if you don't want to do it, you certainly will have friends who will gladly do it for you.

The price of oil has nothing to do with production, refining, delivery, sales, supply and demand: It is the result of speculation by those who can control the price.

Every day, American consumers are hostages of, and robbed by, the world's international oil companies. (It makes you feel sorry for Jesse James: Jesse had to use a gun.)

Too harsh?

Remember a jury awarded a $5 billion judgment against Exxon-Mobil for the 1989 Valdez oil spill? Exxon never paid it. But they did, the next year, take a tax write-off by lowering their estimated oil and gas reserves by $6.1 billion. A nice touch of legal book-keeping . . .

After delaying its way through the federal appeal courts for two decades, in June, 2009, the high court allowed Exxon-Mobil to settle for around $400 million (including interest), an amount less than 10% of the original award.

How long would Exxon-Mobil give you to pay your gas credit card charges?

And would they settle for .08% on the dollar?

But it's not just Exxon: The oil and gas conglomerates have reported increased profits and increased earnings for years, while crying "shortages" and "world demand" and "uncertainties in oil-producing areas".

Besides the CEO's, can you guess who are the happiest?

Think hedge funds, brokerage houses, and investors who can spend $1.4 billion dollars for the shares of one stock.

Oh, yes. In 2005, at least 27-different investors were each holding that much or more in Exxon-Mobil stock.

And for one of the investors, Goldman-Sachs sold $1.4 billion dollars in Exxon stock in one transaction.

And politicians talk about job creation and the economy, while there are no small economic opportunities...

An objective examination of what is going on in the oil and gas world shows that Big Oil took W. C. Fields' advice to heart: "Never give a sucker an even break!"

Heavy Oil -

Oil is judged on its API gravity.

Well, (please excuse), basically, the oil market is based on West Texas Crude, which has an API gravity of 38-40. It is fairly light. In 1859, the oil that Col. Drake pulled out of the ground in Pennsylvania had API gravity near 60, even a lighter and easier-to-pump oil.

The lighter the oil, the easier it is to pump and transport.

Most of the world's oil is of much lower gravity; a heavy, viscous hydrocarbon with very little flow — defined as API gravity 22.3 or less — is costly to produce and difficult to refine. This is why for the past 150-or so years, oil companies have produced the lighter stuff.

But heavy oil has been used. During World War II, the Russians utilized heavy oil deposits, and the Japanese used heavy oil deposits in Japan, Indochina and Indonesia. After the war, when the supplies of lighter crude oil became available once again, these deposits languished.

There is a lot of heavy oil in the world, which means there is a lot of money to be made. And with politics, macroeconomics, monopolies, Smart phones, cheaper investment dollars, all boiling together in a world-wide mix, it is now getting serious consideration.

And newer technology makes it much easier to develop and refine this heavier oil.

And technology is the driving force in "fracking", the new oil play by a new breed of "wildcatter" in the search for energy.

And watch what will happen: Once energy fields have proven to be profitable, the independent and smaller players in the "fracking" side of things will go the route of the oil wildcatters in the 70's. Investors will demand their money. Banks will foreclose. And the majors will force these independent operators out of business or gobble them up.

And when they do, Big Oil will resume its play-full ways with your money.

According to Schlumberger, only about 30% of the total world oil resource is the conventional, light crude. By comparison, heavy oil makes up about 40% of the world's oil resource. The remaining 30% of the world's oil resource is in the form of tar sands and bitumen, and doesn't flow at all.

(One of the largest tar sands developments is in Alberta, Canada, a $500 billion example that currently yields nearly two million barrels of oil per day.)

According to Schlumberger's estimates, there are between 6-9 TRILLION barrels of *known* heavy oil in the world. Based on current rates of total oil world demand of about 30 billion barrels per year, this means around 200-300 years' worth of potential supply.

Where is all of this heavy oil? Here are the nations with the largest estimated deposits:

Country	Oil (in barrels):
Canada	1,760 billion
Russia	1,250 billion
Venezuela	1,200 billion
Kuwait	665 billion
Iraq	380 billion
United States	200 billion
China	180 billion

Other countries with significant heavy oil deposits include Brazil, Indonesia, Australia, South Africa, Nigeria, Peru, Vietnam, and others.

In several countries, China, Russia Peru, Vietnam, Argentina, Brazil, etc., as more is known of deposits they likely will surpass estimates.

Arguments are made that not near all this currently underutilized resource can be tapped. This argument utilizes an obvious point to obfuscate the fact that heavy oil is an immense source of energy. What the world has is years and years of energy resources.

Today, technology allows Chevron to lift about 80,000 barrels per day of heavy oil from its large complex

(8,000 wells) at Kern River, California. Venezuela produces about 400,000-500,000 barrels of heavy oil per day from projects in the Orinoco region. British Petroleum has several billion barrels of heavy oil located near the conventional oil fields of Prudhoe Bay, Alaska. And Brazil's oil company is looking at a massive off-shore heavy oil development.

But primarily all we're doing with heavy oil is finding out where it is...

Why? Because we don't need heavy oil now.

Presently, light crude oil inventories are at their highest levels in two decades. Demand has fallen to a 10-year low. Refineries are operating at less than 85% capacity. Oil company profits continue to achieve new profit highs. But the national price of a gallon of gasoline has climbed around 70-cents a gallon since the first of 2009.

Goldman Sachs & Company, Morgan Stanley, MF Global, the Oil Companies themselves, and other speculators are distorting the process, side-stepping the regulations, placing hardships on consumers, while politicians work to be re-elected.

Until the oil companies can make as much profit as they do from light oil on another source of energy, the other source will never see a widespread market.

Just as all the conglomerates are primarily doing with heavy oil, all they're doing with geothermal and other energy sources, is making sure they'll work.

And any alternative energy source will only be discovered – *known* - when it is as profitable as oil and gas.

Brewed Crude (and other stuff and things)

Lately, a lot of people are thinking about the price of gasoline or home heating costs. Few of us think about that barrel of crude oil, which for the last decade has sold between the low-50's to 100-dollars per barrel..

Well, let's look at brewed crude.

First, a barrel of crude oil only contains 42-gallons, not the 55-gallons we normally think of in measuring a barrel. But refining can turn those 42-gallons of crude into a lot of different products.

According to The American Petroleum Institute, based on 1995 averages at U.S. refineries, here is where an average barrel of oil at American refineries goes in gallons:*

>Gasoline: 19.5 Gallons
>Distillate fuel oil (diesel & home heating): 9.2 Gallons
>Kerosene-type jet fuel: 4.1 Gallons
>Lubricants: 0.5 Gallons
>Residual fuel oil (including industry, marine transportation and electric power generation): 2.3 Gallons
>Petrochemical feedstocks: 1.2 Gallons
>Liquefied refinery gasses: 1.9 Gallons
>Asphalt and road oil: 1.3 Gallons
>Still gas, Coke, & other: 4.0 Gallons
>** Total is greater than 42-gallons because of what the industry calls "processing gain."*

Apologists for Big Oil like to compare the gallon costs of gas to unrelated products, such as bottled water, milk or orange juice. Sorry, people. Have you changed your vehicle oil lately?

Motor oil is just a part of the refining process; and 42-gallons (a barrel) of 5 to 20-weight refined oil brings in approximately $375 at an average retail price. Is this a reasonable mark-up pricing or price gouging?

The apologists also point to the costs of refineries, transportation and storage.

Tuffy wuffy!

Most refineries in the U.S. are over 30-years old. They've paid for themselves several times, over and over and over and over. Same for transportation and shipping: The tankers, trucks and pipelines pay for themselves time after time after time. And storage tanks are never used just *one* time . . .

One energy apologist expert, explaining why we don't have more refineries, said, "Today, the cost of building a new refinery could be almost $3 billion dollars." Well, just *break my heart!!!*

In the first quarter of 2005, Exxon-Mobil's profit *exceeded $7 billion.* A responsible company could have built two $3 billion refineries and still shown a profit. After paying the $38 million annual salary to their head honcho.

Big Oil is a conglomerate of related corporations in an incestuous relationship.

Government provides tax relief, such as depletion allowance, allows book-keeping and accounting tricks, and given a host of special incentives by paid-for-politicians. That individual you elected to office damn sure is not protecting you from enemies within (or likely outside) our national boundaries.

There are more levels of pay in a barrel of oil than there are Big Oil companies.

Azerbaijan approved British Petroleum to tap into that country's rich oil deposits. Many experts consider the Azerbaijan oil field, just one of several oil deposits in the former Soviet Russia, to hold enough oil to meet over one-third of the world's present demands.

To secure the right to Azerbaijan's oil resources, about 25% of all known oil reserves, BP joined with the Azerbaijan and Georgian Oil Companies, which many consider to be a group of thugs, to construct a $3 billion pipeline thru the two countries and Turkey.

At the end of WW II, Russia made a strong play in the Middle East, establishing favorable relations with many of the Arab countries. Their reason for doing so was that the Soviet Russian states were considered to be woefully lacking in oil and gas resources. Only shortly before the breakup of the Soviet brand of communism were large fields of oil and gas discovered in many of the member states.

These recent discoveries have placed the area as one of the world's most promising oil reserves.

(*"Known oil reserves"* is an oil term with a truly flexible real meaning: Of course, estimated *"known reserves"* are known. But with amazing frequency, Big Oil announces "discovery" of another field, such as the one in the former Soviet states. And *"known reserves"* vary: For instance, shortly after the Valdez spill, Exxon changed their "known reserves": They reduced on paper around $6 billion of their *"known reserves"*, which also allowed a very advantageous accounting change that made the write-down a tax loss.)

The BP/Azerbaijan pipeline used approximately 150,000 joints of massive pipe; enough to manufacture a half million cars or 100,000 ocean-going oil tankers. Completed, the pipeline flows an estimated $1.5 billion weekly. Not just for one time, but weekly, year after year after year after year. . .   A massive return on investment.

The pipeline was being built underground, and it's been reported that a sizeable hunk of the $3 billion went as payoffs to as many as 800 corrupt political and hastily-formed oil-related organizations in the three countries.

Supply is not the problem.

An oil monopoly is not the problem.

The problem is a U. S. Congress working for Big Oil.

Oil Speculators and the Big Oil Hoax

"Drill, Baby, Drill" is a hoax: The world is awash in oil.

This we've said since the first artificially-created oil shortage in the early 1970s.

In the spring of 2008, oil prices were increasing, on their way to a then-record of $147 a barrel.

In June of that year, Reuters, the liberal news-gathering organization, helped the Obama campaign for the White House along with an article showing the Presidential candidate in a positive glow.

Candidate Obama said in the article that, if elected President, he would stop the increases in fuel costs by cracking down on speculators in the energy markets.

Obama said he would close the "Enron Loophole" that exempted most large energy traders from regulations in the Commodities Futures markets. (He knew then, and he knows now ... but he's a politician.)

This "Enron Loophole" came with the *"Commodities Modernization Act of 2000."* Those pushing this bit of legislation claimed it was to "modify and modernize" the market. But, actually, it was a wonderful bit of now-you-see-it-now-you-don't government magic.

The purpose of "modernization" was to let speculators (traders) bet on oil prices with little money down, electronically, with such activity not reported and not regulated by any trade authorities.

It was and is legislation to keep such trades "in the dark" – hidden outside public scrutiny.

It is the purest form of special-interest politics. It puts the interest of Big Oil and Big Oil Speculators, many who are "friends" of Big Oil, before the interest of the American public.

Speculators can leverage bid prices on a high volume of oil with little to no money of their own at risk, which extends the price impact on oil. A little bit of borrowed money can create huge returns when bet on a sure thing.

As an example, to trade a crude oil contract on the New York Mercantile Exchange (NYMEX) a trader is only required to maintain a margin that is approximately 8% of the face value of the contract – roughly 8-cents for every dollar. The margin amount will change in different market conditions, but the amount of leverage margins provide makes it attractive for those looking to gain exposure to oil prices.

Artificial shortages, as reported by Big Oil *friendliest* friends – whether natural occurrence or manmade catastrophes; political riots or change in governments; oil shortages or an oil surplus – are the manipulator's excuse for wide swings in oil prices. Insider speculators profit, as every excuse, either negative or positive, is first reported by Big Oil to their friends (with a little lead-in time for their other speculating friends to make their investing plans).

When there is always something you can manipulate – that you can spin the way you want it spun – to impact prices, speculation is not speculative, it is a sure money bet (up and down).

The "Commodities Modernization Act of 2000" was and is a bipartisan sellout of the American public. It was developed and signed off on and continues to have support in both houses of Congress.

"Drill, Baby, Drill" is a hoax: The world is awash in oil. Oil companies who control the supply of oil can't sell all that is available. And if a shortage cannot be sold to the public through manipulation by the nation's know-nothing news media, the companies can always "cut" production – if only in reports.

The only real shortage they can create is in gasoline (over the past 30-years, Big Oil has closed dozens of

U.S. refineries). So, without refining capacity. . .where do you get the gas?

Excessive speculation, coupled with inside information at Big Oil, is the reason for high oil prices, not the real world supply and demand of oil.

Commodities are traded based on margin (the amount of equity a customer is required to have, as a percentage of the current market value of the securities held in the account), and the margin changes based on market volatility and the current face value of the contract.

Since passage of the nation's Commodities Futures Modernization Act of 2000, the world's storage has been overflowing with supply, but prices continue to climb. The weasels tell consumers that oil-demand justifies the price, but speculators have more to do with price than supply.

The fact is, the Commodities Futures Modernization Act allows an unregulated market to manipulate the price of oil. Fraud is difficult to prove, because there is no one governing commodities trading, and friends protect friends; just as politicians protect large contributors to campaigns.

What a gullible public fails to understand is that the oil market is an exception to most political upheavals, which are so beloved by Big Oil and their friends the speculators. Oil producers are not tied to the politics of any one particular region, and neither are oil markets. But any political upheaval, large or small, for any reason, is an excuse to raise prices.

Every day, massive amounts of money, combined with non-supply/demand-based "bids" for oil, flow into the commodity market. And it is all that money and those irrational bid prices, not an insufficient supply of oil, that drives prices.

What most of us have forgotten, oil futures trading only started in 1983: The first trade of West Texas oil was at the New York Mercantile Exchange on March 30, 1983, at 9.30 am Eastern Time.

(This was part of the switch to State Capitalism, which has done so much to ruin our economy – and the lives of millions.)

Crude oil benchmarks, also known as oil markers, followed in the mid 1980s. And oil would never rest again.

The rush to open speculation on oil prices in the commodities market came from the artificial "oil shortages" of the mid-1970s orchestrated by America's oil companies.

Prior to the seventies, oil prices were steady, with most states limiting the pumping of oil to five to seven days a week. This limited pumping came into being at the request of oil companies when, in the 1930s, oil was selling as low as 10-cents a barrel. By limiting the pumping of oil, limiting the supply, a price could be managed that would provide the companies a reasonable profit.

Eventually, oil companies began to chaff at limitations, which they had requested be imposed on them for their protection, seeing a way to make more profit.

During the artificial "oil shortages" of the mid-1970s, orchestrated by America's oil companies, natural gas supplies and prices followed.

And talk of "deregulation" sprung up like daffodils through the snow (job) in Washington, D. C., by oil operatives and oil friends in public office.

At that time, we warned that giving monopolies a seat at the table would be the wrong thing to do. Placing oil in the commodity markets, we warned, would draw inside traders and speculators like vultures to rotten meat.

We were right, not that our forecast was a big deal, but we could not – and still do not – understand how others (except the politically-connected) could fail to see the future consequences of such action.

Natural gas prices (and reported supplies), along with oil, were being manipulated, which in turn, caused electric rates to skyrocket in national markets. Increases in the price for natural gas and heating oil were a deliberate course of action: They allowed the using of natural gas as the excuse for arguing that it and oil should be placed in commodity markets.

And then America lost all reason.

Thirty years of deregulation of the financial services industry, a closed monopoly available for speculation, repeal of the Glass-Steagall Act, The Commodities Futures Modernization Act of 2000, and other similar legislative favors for the Big Money Boys have brought us to the edge of ruin.

All together, these "favors for special interests" have helped turn our economic system from one of Private Enterprise to State Capitalism.

Political and Wall Street geniuses are willing to destroy America in exchange for short-term economic gains ...

and our political and economic leaders know it. Or they should know it. But as long as they can gain power and money from participating in a system of economic enslavement to a favored constituency, they will do nothing to correct a headlong approach to America's economic destruction.

Why would those who are responsible for the fraud and manipulation that are the key economic issues of the day want to change what they're doing?

There is no legitimate reason for State Capitalism, nor are there legitimate reasons for oil prices to be where they are –

Allowing a monopoly in the futures market is opening a door to wrong-doing – unless you can get your legislative friends to pass a law to say it is okay. But it isn't.

Like many other things in America's new State Capitalism.

Today there is plenty of oil. The inventories are at near-record levels and storage is overflowing. Plus, there is no sign of growth in oil consumption: there's plenty of oil, too much for buyers to want it all, but the price has so many ups-and-downs consumers stay seasick.

The only answer to WHY is speculation in the oil markets – a place where bets on oil should never been permitted – is that, too often, we're told things by people who think their breath don't stink.

And it may not.

But their politics certainly do. . .

But back in the land of Crooks, Bankers and Politicians, there is a mindless dream of another world that has only been known in the dreams of those soaked in the mad hope of socialism ... and an excess of self-esteem.

Today, all the political criminally-insane are not in state and federal institutions. Some are teaching at our colleges and universities, and one or two may be instructing at your local high school.

This isn't just un-substantiated speculation; it's the verifiable reality.

And truth comes, as stated by Melville, *"covertly and by snatches."*

Consequently, shouldn't we be asking what special and unique ability do the progressives have that makes them think they know what is best for each of us? And why is that only government can achieve it?

We see the failure of the State Capitalism forced on us.

And as Shakespeare wrote: *"Confusion now hath made his masterpiece."*

If the future is important you have to work for it.

If you leave it for the crooks, bankers and politicians, *you* won't have one.

ABOUT THE AUTHOR

Jake Street is an interpreter of issues and values pertaining, but not limited, to politics, government, and economics as they emerge in American history and culture.

His past life as *The World's Second Greatest Disk Jockey*, chamber of commerce manager, community and economic (and water resources) development consultant, and developer of real estate, provide an indication of a somewhat eclectic blend of experience.

Jake takes things seriously, but never takes himself too seriously. In fact, his sense of humor, and a jaundiced view of false pomposity, is one of his greatest attributes.

Along with a number of magazine and website articles, *Political Fiddle-faddle* is his second book. A new one, *Crooks, Bankers & Politicians* is scheduled for release soon. Jake is currently at work on a new book regarding popular culture and the political scene.

www.ingramcontent.com/pod-product-compliance
Lightning Source LLC
Chambersburg PA
CBHW070250190526
45169CB00001B/352